Rock-Medicine

Rock-Medicine

Earth's Healing Stones from A to Z

A Guide to the Practical Use of Rocks, Crystals & Gemstones

SELA WEIDEMANN RANDAZZO

with contributions by ELAINE NELSON

BLUE DOLPHIN

Published by
Blue Dolphin Publishing, Inc.
P.O. Box 8, Nevada City, CA 95959
http://www.bluedolphinpublishing.com
Orders: 1-800-643-0765

ISBN: 1-57733-024-2

Library of Congress Cataloging-in-Publication Data

Randazzo, Sela Weidemann, 1957–
rock-medicine / Sela Weidemann Randazzo.
v. <1– > cm.
Includes biobliographical references and index.
ISBN 1-57733-024-2 (alk. paper)
1. Crystals—Therapeutic use. 2. Crystals—Psychic aspects. 3. Precious stones—Therapeutic use. 4. Medicine, Magic, mystic and spagiric. I. Title.
RZ415.W45 1998
615.8'9—dc21 97-46814
CIP

Cover art: Peter Teekamp
Cover layout: Lito Castro

Printed in the United States of America

10 9 8 7 6 5 4 3 2 1

Dedication

This book is dedicated to all who hoped that
the Creator of Love would intervene—
from those who believed It would.

Acknowledgments

THE CONTENTS OF THIS BOOK are just the beginning of a new era in technology coming forth for humanity and our planet. This knowledge has come into being through the prayers and desires of all the multitudes who have preceded us throughout time. I wish to thank them for their dreams.

I thank all of you who have supported me in this work over the years, especially those who have cared enough about themselves to use Rock-Medicine faithfully. Without your efforts we would never have seen how consistently successful these methods are.

Elaine and I wish to extend grateful thanks to our families and many friends for their kindness and support.

And our deepest appreciation to Blue Dolphin Publishing for their vision.

Contents

Acknowledgments vi

Introduction xi

Methods of Application 1

Clearing the Stones • 3

The Four Methods • 4

Hand-Held Method • 5

Essence Method • 7

Focus Direct • 10

Blanket Spread • 12

Working with Combinations 15

About the Combinations • 17

Starting with the Master Blend • 19

Adding Specific Combinations • 20

The Master Blend • 21

Shield Stones • 23

The Seven Cleansers • 24

Women's Hormonal Balance Formula • 25

Men's Hormonal Balance Formula • 25

The Stones 27

Abalone • 31

Adamite • 32

Agate • 34

Alexandrite • 35
Amazonite • 37
Amber • 39
Amethyst • 41
Apatite • 43
Aquamarine • 45
Aragonite • 46
Aventurine • 48
Azurite • 50
Azurite/Malachite • 52
Barite • 54
Beryl • 55
Bloodstone • 56
Bornite • 57
Calcite • 59
Carnelian • 61
Celestite • 62
Chalcedony • 64
Chrysocolla • 65
Chrysoprase • 68
Cinnabar • 70
Citrine • 72
Clay • 73
Coal • 75
Coral • 77
Covellite • 78
Diamond • 80
Dinosaur Bone • 82
Emerald • 83
Fluorite • 85
Fluorite Wands • 86
Galena • 88
Garnet • 90

Gold • 92
Granite • 94
Halite • 95
Hematite • 97
Hemimorphite • 98
Herkimer Diamond • 99
Iolite • 100
Ivory • 101
Jacinth/Hessonite Garnet • 102
Jade • 103
Jasper • 105
Kunzite • 106
Lapis Lazuli • 107
Lava • 110
Lepidolite • 112
Magnetite • 114
Malachite • 116
Moldavite • 118
Moonstone (Labradorite) • 119
Mother-of-Pearl • 121
Obsidian • 122
Onyx • 124
Opal • 125
Pearl • 126
Peridot • 129
Petrified Wood • 131
Pyrite • 132
Quartz Crystal
  Clear • 134
  Rose • 137
  Smoky • 139
Red Rock of Sedona • 141
Rhodochrosite • 143

Rhodonite • 144
Ruby • 146
Selenite • 148
Shark's Tooth • 149
Silver • 150
Sodalite • 152
Sugelite • 153
Sulfur • 154
Talc • 155
Tiger's Eye • 156
Topaz • 157
Tourmaline • 158
Turquoise • 160
Ulexite • 161
Wood Opal • 162
Wulfenite • 163

Afterword: The Great Work 165

Appendices 169
Use Guide by Stone • 171
Use Guide for Specific Conditions • 174
Cautions & Safeguards • 179
How to Order Stones • 181
Rock Reference Guides • 181

About the Author 183

Introduction

THE BASIC PREMISE AND INTENTION of this book is to provide both a layman's "use guide" and a comprehensive medical text on the proper use and application of crystals and gemstones as tools for wellness.

These minerals are precision instruments capable of balancing one's mind, body, and spirit to a state of "well being." As the human being is a delicate equation of all three, it is necessary to treat all three areas simultaneously when one is out of balance. As we are three bodies in one, the spiritual, the mental, and the physical, we must understand that imbalance, as well as healing, takes place in the spiritual body first, then the mental, and finally the physical.

All forms of imbalance equate to toxicity, which in turn manifests as illness. We have not, as yet, perfected methods of diagnosing and treating precisely the imbalances that take place in the spirit. We have just begun to uncover the means of addressing the imbalances of the mind. This makes our physical body the main focus when searching for healing.

You will probably find my personal story just as hard to believe as I do—and I'm the one who lived it. All my life I have felt that I would do something special. In fact, at the age of five, I asked God to let me help this planet. The televised scenes of children starving, skeleton-like, in the television fund-raisers, caused me to really mean it. I grew to believe that my contribution would probably be in the field of politics, since no other arena measured up to my inspiration for change. Little did I realize that what the Creator had in mind would literally "rock" nations.

I can remember a significant paranormal experience at age five. Not many conscious memories exist for me any earlier than that, and that fact is probably the best validation I have of the change that took place at that time, which caused me to become someone different, a "walk-in," you might say. I can tell you the details of the very night it happened.

I was at the house of my best friend. Her name was Maureen. She and I were in her family's recreation room playing ping-pong. All of a sudden, in mid-swing, I was stopped short by a clearly audible voice saying, "Your mother wants you home." I knew immediately that neither Maureen, nor her brother or father, who were also in the room, had spoken. Nor had they heard it. I said aloud, "My mother wants me home." This was not a statement that would cause any of them to be aware of what had and was taking place. As I lived close by, I set off alone for home. It was dusk. Night was falling fast. A combination of night blindness and dyslexia had me turned around and lost in minutes.

My parents had raised us intelligently, and I knew my full name and address. I was not afraid. I also knew that I was in my own neighborhood. All the houses around me were my neighbors'. I went up to the closest doorway and knocked. No answer. Now it was dark. Instead of it occurring to me to try the next door, I panicked and felt very frightened.

I turned from the door and bolted toward the first of four steps leading to the sidewalk. As soon as I was at the edge of that top step, I bumped into someone standing there. I looked up to see the face of Jesus. His was the familiar face and garb from every Sunday school picture I'd ever seen. He was just standing there. I was raised by a fanatically fundamentalist mother. With this intense Biblical orientation, the stories and miracles were real to me, and I had been deeply ingrained with the perception of Jesus as a real human being who was my friend. In that light, my gut level reaction was one of relief. I knew, in my understanding of the situation, that if I was lost, Jesus was probably a very good person to have show up. There was no verbal communication, but I felt His mind search mine. At the moment He established that I was comfortable with the persona that stood before me, He was no longer the same. All of a sudden He was not the familiar Christian manifestation but rather a total Light Being. In the next moment, I was caught up in His arms and instantaneously in front of my own front door.

My mother was a mentally unbalanced woman whose illness went undetected among her fanatical religious organizations. My father was a lawyer, a chemist, and an electrical engineer. In fact, he was the individual who formulated unleaded gasoline at Atlantic Richfield Laboratories.

From that day and for about the next three years, I found myself in a frequent state of tears. I remember sitting at the dinner table, crying from such a profoundly deep place. My parents would ask me what was wrong. I could only answer them by saying that I could not explain it, but that everything was really going to be all right. It was as if I were detached from my feelings. Although I was crying big crocodile tears, I did not feel sadness in my heart but rather duty. This, I later learned, is known as travail, the agonizing over the plight of all humankind.

The next major incident in this saga occurred when I was eight years old. We were members of a Pentecostal church in downtown Philadelphia, the City of Brotherly Love. While in the midst of listening to a Sunday morning sermon, as I looked around the sanctuary, I saw every person in the building light up. They were like individual lights on a Christmas tree, each person with a color surrounding their body. The effect was so vivid and obvious that it did not occur to me that I was the only one seeing it. I elbowed my mother and said, "Look at that!" She responded quizzically and asked what I was talking about. I didn't take my eyes off the illuminated crowd and said, "That! . . . Everyone is lit up with color!" She again asked what I was talking about. I was so frustrated by the possibility that she did not see it, that I responded with exasperation, "Our minister is glowing with a lime green light!"

The next thing I knew I was being rushed down the aisle to the altar. This was not to cast the demons out of me but rather to proclaim me as a child prophet. I was learning that it was not the best idea to let anyone know what was happening to me—that you do not let other people know when these things happen. We ended up at the preacher's home for dinner. He got to revel in his color, and Mother got to be in the special holy spotlight. I was disgusted. I was torn between the comfortable absurdity of my mother's church group and the knowledge that I was being singled out for incredible communication with our Creator. I chose to be temporarily sucked in by the promise of rapture, or at the very least, salvation. I even took my ten dollars of birthday money and gave it all to the collection plate the following Sunday. It took me three tries to be certain that I had the minister's eye as I gave it. This, however, was definitely my mistake. In the instant that my gift was realized from the pulpit, I knew that the value of what I had offered was lost, for I was giving for the value's sake and not for the giving's sake.

The feeling of specialness dwindled in the years between eight and ten. Then, one late fall day, it was reborn. My older sister, her best friend, and I were dragging a bale of hay home to our dog's house, across a field, in our wagon. As we reached the center of the open field, all of a sudden we were aware of a ship—a space ship. It hovered perfectly still, only sixty feet above our heads. It was so close that the detail is still deeply embedded in my memory. When we looked up, we all saw the underbelly of the ship clearly. We had been walking in daylight when we left the farm with the hay. Now we were looking up through pitch darkness at the lights and siding of a spacecraft. If there were rivets connecting the individual panels of metal, we could have seen them. However, there were neat seams and no rivets. This encounter was so spectacularly close that the three of us did not speak about it for almost ten years.

At the time, my sisters and I were living through a nightmare of physical and mental abuse. What we did not fear from my mother, we feared from her ever more radical church groups. Fortunately for me, I had the benefit of an audible voice guiding me, but to this day the results of our cruel childhood can still be seen vividly in my three sisters. It is as if someone altogether different raised me. They did.

When my father died, I was thirteen and had recently been allowed to have my own room, for I was always the one who had had to share a room with one of my sisters. The night my father died, I was in my bed. Movement in a picture of the little shepherd boy caught my attention, as it all of a sudden became animated, lifelike, with subtle movement by the boy and the lamb in his arms. As my attention was drawn to the picture, I did not notice from where my father came, but became suddenly aware of his full physical presence at my bedside. He said in a telepathic way that he had been allowed to come and say good-bye, only to me. As I rose up out of my bed, he said I may not touch him. I followed him down the hallway from my room, but instead of turning the corner as usual, he disappeared into the wall. The fact that I had risen up out of bed to participate in this encounter let me know that it was an actual occurrence and not a dream.

Just a few months later, my sisters and I found ourselves on a fifteen-acre religious cult campground. Our mother told us that we were there for a three-week camp. One month later she informed us that our estate in Pennsylvania had been put up for sale, and we were going to live here. We were registered into the local school. I was moved from seventh to ninth grade and began cutting school four out of five days a week, while remaining an "A" student. We girls were four little princesses moved from absolute wealth to abject poverty. The two-room cabin we moved into had no indoor plumbing, and we had to navigate a swamp and an electrified pony fence to reach the outhouse.

The voice that I had heard since the age of five on a daily basis had never left me, but it was not until the age of sixteen that I realized that not everyone was hearing this voice. This comforting voice never told me anything strange or harmful. It taught me that having a physically and mentally abusive parent was not the consequence of my being good or bad but rather of my mother being ill.

The campground experience was one continuous nightmare of physical and emotional abuse, with the majority of abuse coming from my mother or with her sanctioning. At the age of sixteen, I finally left home and went out into the world on my own. The spirit continued to speak to me.

Sela Weidemann was the name given me at birth. Literally, it means "rock shepherd." However, this fact did not come to my attention until many years after my work with the mineral kingdom had begun.

Fifteen years ago, I attended a conference in Detroit on metaphysics. As I was a novice to such topics as advanced astrology, numerology, and the Tarot, I opted to sit in on the only presentation being offered to a beginning student. The subject matter was healing with gemstones and was presented by a woman from Larkspur, California. The method by which we were taught to determine appropriate usage of the individual stones is called "kinesiology," or muscle testing, a widely used and accepted testing method among physicians and therapists. In simple terms, the subject's own muscle strength or weakness is used to obtain accurate indications from his or her subconscious, regarding which substances may be contraindicated for use due to allergy, for example, or even decisions regarding business, health, or relationship.

After about five years of utilizing this practice, I began to see combinations of stones being indicated consistently for the same maladies. Over time, constant cross-referencing gave me a standardization for the use of about thirty stones.

Early in 1987, I spontaneously began "channeling," or receiving audibly, the specific usages of another seventy or so stones. This gracious intervention by a "higher source of knowledge" was, in effect, an emergency measure. The Creator saw that we as a people have all but destroyed our earthly kingdom and ourselves along with it. The polluting of our waters, air, and soil have rendered the vegetable kingdom toxic, and we cannot treat something toxic with something toxic.

The plant life from which we derive most of our medicinal products is becoming virtually useless as a means by which we can obtain health. This catastrophe is echoed in the headlines. Mainstream medicine offers the explanation that our bodies are setting up immunities to common medica-

tions, when in fact it is the toxins from the raw materials used to make them that they attempt to combat. Then, with the onset of the atomic age, we began also to put our mineral kingdom at risk through the effects of radiation. The mineral kingdom is our last available source of medicine for healing ourselves and the planet. This is a conclusion that clinical science will reach eventually by itself, but not before too much damage is done to the Earth's mineral resources. As a result of these circumstances and my request to be of assistance, the art and science of Rock-Medicine was born.

The mineral kingdom is now being recognized as a viable means of healing, and history substantiates this kingdom's work record. The very names of individual stones sometimes were given them because of their healing virtues. We see countless examples of ancient Egyptian tombs safeguarding the remains of the dead, as well as the amulets and beads that were used to treat them while alive. Prophetic references to the mineral kingdom, both past and present, are well-documented in virtually all teachings of theology and alchemy.

It is my firm belief that the ancient loss of the practical use of these instruments was due to the greed of those to whom the original knowledge was imparted. It is also my belief that the Biblical reference to Christ's words concerning the "rocks and stones crying out to bear witness to the power of the Creator, at a time when humankind has ceased to glorify creation," is speaking about the resurgence of Rock-Medicine, as introduced here and now.

There is no mystery here. This volume presents all the information received to date. Many more stones and their uses remain to be learned. However, the maladies chosen to be addressed first, herein, are a composite of our world's current needs and heaven's own priorities.

This information comes at a time when many great minds are working to unite our hearts and turn our convictions toward true unconditional love, a source of harmonious delight, where happiness, health, and camaraderie manifest as the combined riches of Heaven on Earth. This planet has provided for the survival of life, here. Our conscientious use of the available tools guarantees the quality of that life.

Introducing Rock-Medicine into the daily lives of us all can be likened to a purge of fire, for the vast mineral kingdom represents the molten veins of the early formation of the Earth. These "rocks" were born at a time that well predates man's polluting of the environment by thought, word, and deed. With these rocks we can clean it up.

It is my understanding that nothing divine or extraterrestrial can tolerate this soupy mess that we have created, for it was not here the last time they walked among man, and it is not of them. If we expect to have their company, we had better clean up our home, for they cannot get any closer than our farthest point of pollution.

The animal, vegetable, and mineral kingdoms are all relative to one another, as are the mind, body, and soul of an individual. Likewise, each of us is individually reflective to all others. Given this oneness, the health of one affects the wellness of all. This includes All That Is. As the Chinese proverb says, "When the cow in Hunan catches cold, the cow in Szechuan sneezes." Just as the chain is only as strong as the weakest link, so can all of creation only be doing as well as we are. In this light, the logic of evolution presents us with the means to detoxify an extremely toxic existence through the only kingdom (or tools) left untainted—the "rock of ages."

Through Rock-Medicine we can treat the common cold or AIDS. We can use this science as healing or prevention.

The only requirement for these minerals to be effective is that they must be used. The methods are simple and few. For example, essences rendered from gemstones are practically as obtainable and affordable as the water in which they are made.

Stones and rocks have been gathered by many, many people who do not know how they work. This is the best of all possible situations—to have the masses gathering about themselves the cherished means of utilizing vibrational influences, just as the instructions are yet arriving. We did and somehow do recognize this mineral kingdom and its worth. Magic is not a miracle of power, but that of creative desire. When creative desire is given energy, it becomes a manifestation.

You may well ask here why we do not all just use our inherent mental abilities to manifest a peaceful and healthy world? Certainly, that is one way of accomplishing this world goal. Unfortunately, people are too ill of mind, body, and spirit, as a whole, to facilitate the use of their will to bring about these major changes. Stone medicine is the method by which we will heal ourselves to a point of truly utilizing our own individual and collective power to their unlimited potential. In the past, medical science has been hampered in its attempts to standardize treatments and cures. In many cases (cancer and arthritis, for example) we find inconsistency in the effectiveness of the treatments. What sometimes works, but does not always, is an extremely tenuous way to approach healing. However, Rock-Medicine always does its job. The chemical vibrations are a constant.

When properties of any kind converge as a result of the evolution of life, a harmonic occurs. A major harmonic occurrence, on August 17, 1987, marked the birth of the mineral kingdom's vibration for use in the New Age. On that date, a coming together of energy and light was celebrated around the world; many more than understood gathered, danced, prayed, meditated, and participated in a celebration of global harmony. We moved from the Age of Fire into the Age of Light. This action prompted an act of faith and hope for the bonding of the life forces of the planet with new strength and wellness.

Since that moment, many monumental occurrences have caused dramatic change. Unusual global weather patterns and geological motions are being reported to us now on nearly a daily basis. New political freedoms are being orchestrated in Russia, Germany, and the Middle East. The use and observation by the masses of Rock-Medicine will be another milestone among significant events, for a resounding need exists worldwide for a more comprehensive and available means of medical self-help.

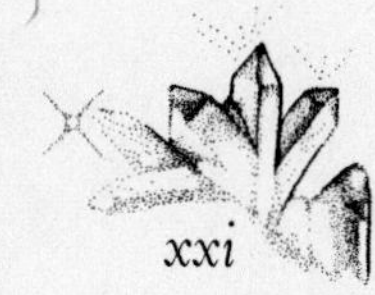

With this new age also came a reorchestration of natural laws governing karma and responsibility. The end of karma as we knew it deems it our responsibility to care for each other in a way we never have done before. Rock-Medicine enables us to treat one another with or without knowledge and with or without permission. It is important to realize that the time is here for us all to be well. All the lessons that we can learn from war, greed, prejudice, and the like, are in place. We can now put these ill energies behind us, in their proper place—let them serve as deterrents for ever returning to those mindsets again. Heaven on Earth is ours to create now.

However, Heaven is not manifested yet. Yes, that's right! It does not exist anywhere, for how can there be Heaven on this plane or on any other, if you or I are not there? The very definition of Heaven invites all to be included. Sure, it's possible to have comfort, even joy, in this life. The happiest one can be, however, falls painfully short of the nirvana that will exist when creation resides in Heaven-space. Humankind has been so far from the Heaven-space for so long that we have actually forgotten its reality. We have taken to deluding ourselves into thinking and teaching that it is a place that exists only in our hearts or minds. Some teach that it is a space reached only after death. Nonetheless, I am certain that my deceased grandmother and father are not sitting in ignorant bliss somewhere while their Sela laments the condition of this world. As long as one child goes to bed on a given night unhugged or unfed, Heaven will not exist for anyone.

When we consider the word "holy," we also get the word "whole." This is the dictionary's interpretation. In other words, all that is not well is ill, and as we all are part of each other and the planet, then no one can truly be well until we all are. Furthermore, the best description of the word "Creator" I can offer is this: the combination of Truth and Self-discipleship always produces a state of unconditional Love. This is the "God is Love" theory. Self-discipleship is being true to one's self or person, true to one's own needs and desires. Self's basic need and desire is health. From this, all happiness is derived.

Finally, no thought or term is more scientific than the word "Truth." There is no greater power on Earth than that of the mind (or self). Enlightenment—the awareness that we are all one and of the same—is Self-discipleship in its truest form.

Right now the planet and its atmosphere are toxic, as are the animal and vegetable kingdoms. Only deep inside the rock of ages do we find untainted vibration. This has been kept safe there for us. All over the world and in every culture are threads of knowledge that have kept conscious connection with this wisdom, until such a time that humankind uses them maturely.

Crystals, rocks, gemstones, fossils, metals, and even crystallized saps, such as amber, make up the vast array of precision vibrational instruments used in Rock-Medicine. As the time-space continuum flows us through the planetary changes, we see antiquation as we advance. This is also true of the applications of the stones. Some, if not most, of the ancient standards are no longer applicable and have evolved into a different correlation to the planet, her atmosphere, and her inhabitants. We find that some minerals have gained in their resonant strength to a point of being a certain danger, if used improperly. When one obtains an awareness as to the proper handling of the mineral influences in one's surroundings, one incurs an automatic obligation to learn the potential risks, safeguards, and antidotes related to these energies. Furthermore, this kingdom is not set up to be used in any heinous or malicious manner.

Rock-Medicine presents aspects of the origin, history, practice, safeguards, essence-making, and methodology of this knowledge. We wish you delight and wisdom as this great work of ours proceeds. We are our own best aspect and resource. A new harmonic created by our repetition of the use of these resources will serve to help reawaken the skills of research, study, and development of cosmic existence. A computerlike higher mind is being linked to us on a conscious level; our socioeconomic convictions bear witness to this. Peace is a popular demand. Peace of mind is happiness, peace of body is health, and peace of soul is freedom. The truest of freedoms is free-flow. Another such evolutionary trend is out-of-body travel. Astral projection is only one of the precursors to our evolving in ourselves the skills of telepathy, teleportation, telekinesis, and astral travel.

In this course, a known truth or conscious truth is called knowledge, but knowledge in itself remains moot until a demonstrative vibration causes it to become wisdom. As cause and effect go, wisdom perpetuates life's survival, growth, and improvement. Loggins and Messina aptly penned, "The wise man has the power. . . ."

Another timely analogy is the phrase from a Van Morrison song, "If I could teach my heart to think and my head to feel. . . ." This is an apt description of the current enlightening process by Spirit. Our hearts' desires are being raised to our minds and are pushing the mental energy flow upward, physically and emotionally. The spirit is doing as well as the mind and body are, and to the same degree.

Many forms of exercise, such as yoga, tai chi, meditation, and the study of chakras to name a few, have been incorporated into the education of being one with all to introduce us to a state of total awareness. The various meditative practices were all for the furthering of our progress toward a state of grace, or a divine state. The harmony of matter is in constant motion. Unfortunately, many of these simple exercises have been built into dogmas, doctrines, and icons of worship instead of the tools they are meant to be.

There are no mantras, prayers, incantations, or ceremonies in the practical application of Rock-Medicine. It is a very simple and basic system. The only action necessary is that the medicine must be used as prescribed. Special care must be used in the sharing of this understanding and practice. We suggest that you read this text in full, and that you use it with a working knowledge, in other words, with wisdom.

Methods of Application

Clearing the Stones

To clear the stones, it is not necessary to do anything but leave them alone. No sunlight, moonlight, or salt cleansing makes any difference. In fact, using salt or salt water is detrimental to your mineral tools, as it has a caustic effect on them. This practice is just an "old wives' tale" and originates from when sages and shamans of old carried their stones and crystals from place to place on their backs with their ration of food and good drinking water. They stopped periodically to wash the dust off. When by the coast, they used the salty sea water as opposed to using their precious drinking water. It was a simple matter of practicality that has been blown way out of proportion.

Just as the blood takes three hours to pass once through our body, and just as our bodies grow a new top layer of skin over a given period of days, so the stones cleanse themselves by completing a full revolution or cycle in their atomic substance in a matter of three hours.

The stones may be put in your pocket or in a bag around your neck to clear, just as long as they are not in direct contact with your skin. They may be put on a shelf, table, or counter. Place them on, or in, any nonmetallic surface, and they will clear themselves in three hours. It is advised that, when clearing them, they not be placed on any appliance that is plugged into an electrical socket.

The Four Methods

There are four main methods of application: 1) *hand-held,* 2) *essence,* 3) *focus direct,* and 4) *blanket spread.* From the first to the fourth, they are in order of greater to lesser ability as far as bringing the most expeditious healing. Hand-holding the stones is the best. Rendering an " essence" is the next most beneficial. A focus direct application is quite a bit slower, as is the blanket spread, which requires months to match results obtained from holding the stones themselves for days.

It is very important to be aware of coming into contact with any other minerals while doing any of these applications. The presence of jewelry can alter the effects. It is particularly important to remove all silver when treating for physical imbalance. Silver or other minerals should be removed for the minutes you are holding the stones or for the moments it takes to drink some essence. The jewelry can be put back on immediately following the application but must again be removed for each subsequent application. All of the shield stones, however, are exempt from this rule, as they work on the etheric body and not on the physical.

Three to four hours after setting the stones to clear, the hand-held twenty-minute treatment is repeated. This is to be done four times each day. Up to six hours may pass between treatments.

The body's most natural method of healing is rest. Therefore, it is not conducive to wellness to interrupt one's sleep to continue this regimen. Four well-spaced applications from rising to bedtime are sufficient.

The best stones to use are rough, uncut, and unpolished. Nonetheless, the first rule of thumb is to "use what you have versus not bringing the healing." Even if your application requires amethyst, for example, an amethyst in a piece of jewelry will do, as long as it is not set in silver.

Hand-Held Method

The hand-held method is the strongest, most expeditious means of administering Rock-Medicine. The stones are held for just under twenty minutes, four times a day. If the time exceeds twenty minutes by even a second, you run the risk of oversaturating, or overmingling, the stones' vibrations with the toxic vibrations they contact in you. The result will be the voiding of that application, but it will not make you any sicker than you were. I find it helpful to set my timer at eighteen minutes to insure against running the treatment too long. Fifteen minutes is the absolute minimum for a hand-held application. After the time is up, set the stones aside to clear.

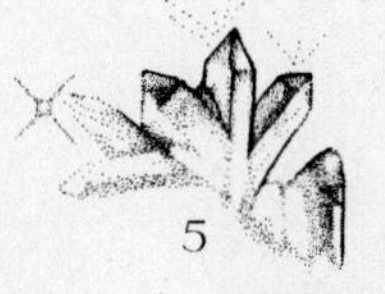

The effect of Rock-Medicine is akin to the way that prescription antibiotics work. When the rock vibration encounters an ailing area, the stone boosts it up to its well point. After three to four hours, it begins dropping back down to an ill or low resonance level. Then you come in with the next application. Over time, these repetitive intervals of help act like a parent helping a child ride his two-wheeler. The balance is learned and eventually holds its own.

The hand-held method is admittedly the most cumbersome application, but it is also the most potent. For the application of the Master Blend cleansing, you will probably want to set a single quartz crystal to the stones, then hold just the crystal as prescribed. The stones must touch each other, and the crystal must touch one or more of them. Holding thirty-three stones at a time can be difficult. Because of the size the stones are required to be, and to fit that many in one hand, the chance of dropping or losing one is increased.

All stones combined for the specific imbalance being addressed are to be held together in the proper hand. For men, the proper hand is the left hand, and for women it is the right. This is consistent with the direction of the body's energy flow. A woman's flow comes in through her right hand and out her left. A man's flow comes in through his left hand and out his right. Regardless of one's sexual orientation, the chromosomal pattern designating male and female is the basis to determine which hand to use. If the patient is not able to hold the stones or take essence, you can use the flow of energy by holding the stones for them and holding their hand. Be mindful of their sex and yours and which direction the flow is going. For example, if you are a woman, you will want to hold the stones in your right hand and use your left hand to hold their hand. Your left hand holds their right hand if they are female. Your left hand holds their left hand if they are male.

Essence Method

It is not necessary to cleanse stones after they have been used to render essences. However, it is very necessary to use cleared stones when beginning to make the *essence*. Also, it is a good idea not to touch the three-hour cleared stones with your bare skin; use plastic gloves or wooden or plastic utensils to transfer stones. The nonreceiving hand for men is the right and for women the left. An essence is rendered by placing cleared stones in a glass bowl, jar, or tumbler filled with water. Plastic containers may be used. However, never use a metal container to render an essence.

The best water to use is purified drinking water as opposed to mineral or spring water, which may contain other chemical substances that can alter the vibrational equation. Distilled water is a good choice. Put your combination in the water for at least three to four hours (the full revolution time), covering the container to prevent dust settling in it, and use common sense to ensure that no residual particles settle into your essence. Three hours later you will notice that all the stones have air bubbles on them. This indicates that each stone has implemented an oxygen exchange, which signifies the rendering of the chemical vibration into the water. Be aware that some stones are water soluble or occur in a powdery or crumbly state, which prohibits their use in an essence. However, you can use a "set" quartz crystal that has been in contact with the required stones for at least three hours, every time you make an essence, if your instrument is water soluble. Then take care to remove any dust or particles from the clear quartz crystal before placing it in the essence water. (See Quartz Crystal, Clear). This ensures that no physical or chemical residue from the minerals is absorbed or ingested.

The stones may then be removed from the water or left in. Whether a bathtub full or a cupful, the water is now full strength essence. Essence must not be diluted by more than fifty percent with water or other liquid. Essence, as well as the two following applications, enables us to treat someone without their even being aware of the application, and this works just as well as if they were to use it for themselves. The addict, the angry, the mean, the prejudiced, the nonbeliever in wellness, and all other types of self-destructive imbalances are all circumstances that can be addressed. If a person does not desire to be well, they represent the best case for treating someone without their permission or conscious involvement. In such a case, essence may be added to any beverage that may be safely ingested.

Now, there are many who buy into the classic laws of karma and would argue that it is not appropriate to treat under these circumstances. However, if someone were to have a heart attack, we would all run to the phone to dial 911 and would administer CPR in the meantime. How then can we separate such cases from those who are having a mental or spiritual "heart attack" and are not capable of giving their permission for treatment? If a person is not conscious of a lack of wellness, they are obviously ill. In the same way, we may pray for another's benefit, even when the person doesn't know of the prayer. Many medical healings that confound traditional doctors have occurred via the power of prayer, often anonymously.

Essence works well in a baby's bottle. If the patient is required to take nothing by mouth, per physicians' orders, the essence may be applied by drops to the forehead or wrists, although this is not as effective as when ingested. We have had great success with putting the crystals or stones into animals' water dishes. In this way, they get continuous application and have never eaten or swallowed the stones. In fact, we have observed definite preferences on the part of horses when offered multiple identical drinking containers. They exclusively chose to drink out of the barrel with the Rock-Medicine in it, even going to the extent of struggling to get water at a low point in one barrel verses drinking from a higher level of water in another barrel. When the stones were moved to the other barrel, the results were the same.

The standard application of essence is four drops held under the tongue briefly before swallowing. The capillaries under the tongue are very close to the surface and absorb essence quickly into the bloodstream. For eye problems, such as a sty, the essence can be dropped right into the eye. Also, ear infections respond well to the drops being administered directly into the ear. This application is repeated four times a day at the same three-to-six hour intervals, for a minimum of three weeks. This is the minimum requirement. The most efficient method of using the essence is to fill your daily water bottle with it and USE it throughout the day. You cannot get too much of the vibration in the essence, for more ingested does not do more. Likewise, there is no threat of overdosing on this medicine. The same rules apply here as with all applications of Rock-Medicine: the duration of treatment is directly related to the severity and prolongation of the illness.

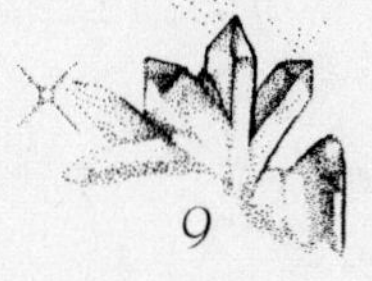

Essence can be stored in an amber or dark-colored dropper bottle, available at most pharmacies. If large volume amounts of essence are made, you may want to refrigerate it to avoid algae growing in the water. Since the Rock Vibration is inorganic, it is not necessary to use any type of catalyst, suspension medium, or preservative. The vibration is forever captured in the water.

Focus Direct

In order to work a *focus direct application,* the first thing required is a quartz crystal with a perfect point. This means it has no chips, no cracks, and no mutilation of any kind. When a stone or stones are set against the base or sides of a clear quartz crystal, the stones' vibrations travel along the body of the crystal, and as in a turbocharger, they are forced into a smaller and smaller space, to be emitted as a "beam" of the individual or collective stones' energy. This laser-like gun can be directed at any individual and will constitute an application of Rock-Medicine. This beam will not travel through walls or glass or turn corners. If anyone steps between the beam and its intended goal, that person will then be its affected target.

If a cluster of quartz crystals are used, a beam will be emitted from each and every perfect point on the cluster. This in fact makes an excellent tool to use in any home, office, classroom, or work place. A focus direct can also be aimed at a bed or therapist's table. This application can be used by teachers, chiropractors, counselors, or anyone desiring to gain assistance while working with others.

Choose the stones to be used in your focus direct application carefully. Use common sense and know exactly what each stone does by referring to the use guides combinations.

The focus direct sends the beam(s) a distance directly proportional to the weight of the piece of quartz used. That distance is approximately 100 feet per pound (50 feet per half pound, 25 feet per quarter pound, and so on).

The focus direct method is much less expeditious in its ability to heal completely than the essence or hand-held method.

Stones used in an essence, focus direct, or blanket spread application need no clearing time, as they are not in physical contact with any toxins. If stones have been held, they must be cleared before using them in any of the other three methods or using them in a hand-held treatment for someone else.

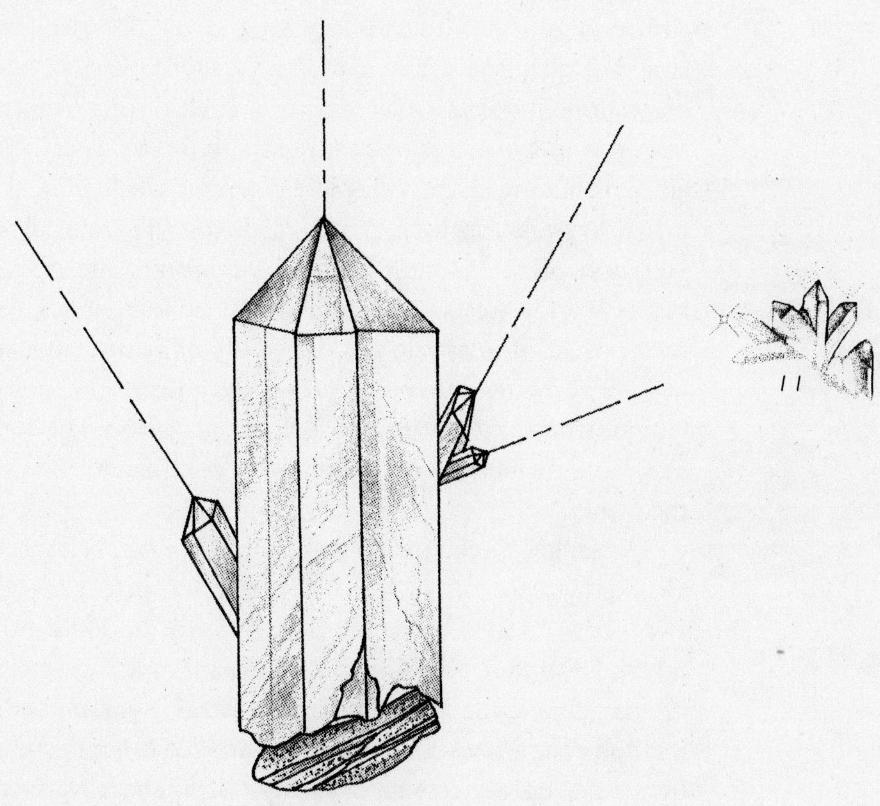

This shows an example of a focus direct. Each perfect point of quartz crystal sends the beam of whatever stone is being generated. A one-pound quartz sends the beam 100 feet; a half-pound quartz sends it 50 feet.

Blanket Spread

The *blanket spread* is also generated through clear quartz crystal. The crystal or crystals used need not be clean or transparent nor have good points or termination. Place stones for combination against the clear quartz crystal on any sides, just as long as all stones touch the crystal(s). Then surround all this with a ring of lapis lazuli. This can be a strand of lapis beads. You may also use single pieces of lapis, placed touching each other, to form a circle or ring. Another option is to use pieces of clear quartz to form the strand or circle, including at least one piece of lapis in the line-up. The quartz crystals touching the other pieces will transmit the vibration of the single piece of lapis around the ring. A blanket spread treats a full radius of one hundred miles from each pound of quartz in the center. Its influence emanates upward, downward, and all around from the spread. The vibration penetrates walls, roofs, floors, and so on. This is the method by which we may treat cities, continents, and even the planet.

A blanket spread may only be set as a general cleansing, an etheric treatment, or an application for a specific malady. In other words, the blanket spread will work (as do the other methods) to treat only one specific malady and must consist of one clear equation at a time. Just as with the other methods, the stones communicate with each other to specify the area being addressed. For example, if you have placed the stones in combination for a back problem with the stones that indicate an eye problem, the vibrations cannot respond to the command to go to two places at the same time.

Rock-Medicine is a precision technology. Just as with some pharmaceutical medicines, treating two different maladies at the same time may not always be advised. You must take differing applications separately. If you are taking essences, you will want to keep the combinations each in their own container, and sip them a few moments apart. Always treat in priority order, beginning with the most serious situation first. You may use one application right after another in this way, but they must be applied in full and separately from one another. When treating physical maladies, this applies to all four forms of application, because the

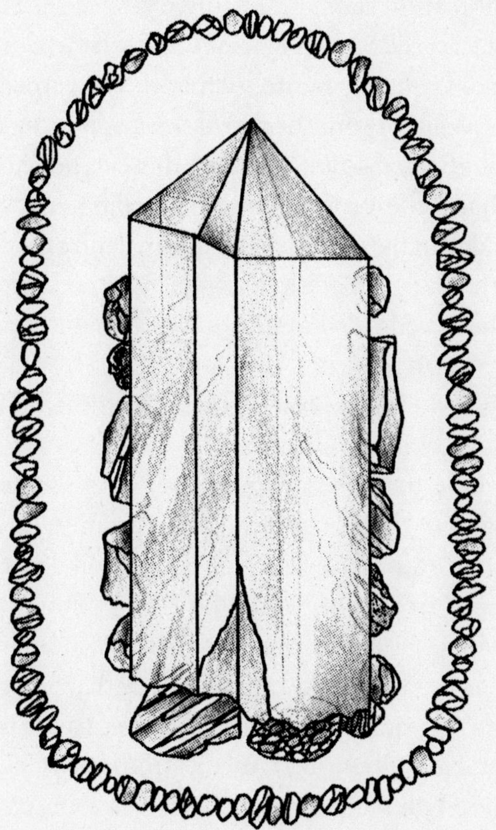

This is an overhead view of a blanket spread. The crystal, stones, and lapis ring are lying flat on a table.

stones work through electromagnetic vibration. In other words, they "speak" to each other, together forming a message for directing the combination, much like letters or numbers. Just as if you were told to go to two places at the same time, the stones are unable to go in any direction when given two different chemical messages simultaneously.

Rock-Medicine combinations form a sentence. Each stone added to that sentence will direct the healing vibration more specifically to what is wrong and where it is located. Every combination starts preferably with the Master Blend, but with at least the Seven General Cleansers, which are jade, amber, smoky quartz, pyrite, hematite (or carnelian), old clay, and covellite. From there you determine which part of the body is affected—tissue, nerve, muscle, bone, or whatever—and add the proper stones accordingly. It is highly recommended in the event of multiple maladies that you start the first three weeks with just the Master Blend which contains the Seven General Cleansers. After the three weeks are up, reevaluate the condition and establish which imbalances remain, and then proceed by treating them in priority order with specific combinations.

Please note that when you first begin to use the stones, your system will experience rapid detoxification on all levels. It is common to have several hours of flu-like symptoms a few days into treatment, as the body will eliminate toxins through whatever orifices are most convenient.

Most important, it is always necessary that you get initial diagnosis from a qualified medical professional. When one is currently taking prescribed medications such as insulin, lithium, blood pressure or thyroid medications, etc., checkups by a physician must be dramatically increased in frequency in order to adjust medication doses as the body heals.

Working with Combinations

About the Combinations

Rock-Medicine works by way of electromagnetic vibration at a chemical level. We are matter in motion. This is grade school science class information. All that exists is composed of minute particles moving at rapid speeds. Though we cannot pass our hand through a tabletop, we know that it actually consists of tiny particles that are constantly moving.

The three life kingdoms on the planet give off electricity when they are alive. It is easy for us to see when the life force has gone out of a plant or animal, for they have lost their electrical charge. On the other hand, the mineral kingdom does not lose its electrical charge, as long as one crystal cell remains intact. This is why we use the stones and minerals themselves, for their ability to give off a chemically based electrical charge. It is not appropriate to alter them by heating, dyeing, or pulverizing them. The whole point in utilizing this medicine is that we can treat ourselves with no residuals, and thus, no side effects. Nor is this medicine meant to be ingested, as Rock-Medicine works via vibration only.

You will notice various groupings of stones referred to throughout this text. Other than the individual combinations for treating specific ailments, the major groupings are the Master Blend, the Shield Stones, and the Seven Cleansers. The Master Blend is appropriate for use by everyone for an initial cleansing. The Shields, which are all included in the Master Blend, may be used individually or in combinations, as temporary or long-term measures. The Seven Cleansers are also all in the Master Blend. If you are treating multiple conditions, you will need to include the Seven Cleansers with all your stone sentences, if the master blend is not used as the base. In other words, if you are treating a heart condition, you will use the Master Blend plus the stones that work with the heart problem. If you are wanting to treat, say, arthritis at the same time, then you need to make a second stone combination for arthritis, including either the Master Blend or the Seven Cleansers. This second application may be performed either before or after the other one.

There are two separate combinations for hormones. Citrine, bornite, and ulexite combine for men's balance, and lapis, opal, and pearl make up the combination for women. The combining of stones is the secret to success after diagnosis. Make sure that you always double-check your combinations.

Another important thing to remember is that the Master Blend addresses the underlying *causes* of (i.e., predispositions to) illness. However, when the Master Blend alone does not prove to fully address a specific imbalance or illness, you need to add stones that "balance the cause/effect equation" and treat the specific symptoms.

$$\frac{\text{to balance cause}}{\text{master blend}} + \frac{\text{to balance effect}}{\text{specifics}} = \text{total balance}$$

Starting with the Master Blend

In the serious pursuit of wellness, it is necessary to treat not only the symptoms of illness but also the causes or catalysts. Over the years we have had many experiences with combining the specific stones for a single malady. In countless instances where the prescribed application was administered, the malady itself would disappear. However, a secondary illness would often surface elsewhere. In treating that second condition, we often found the process repeated itself, again revealing a subsequent illness.

This led us to the obvious conclusion that we were not addressing the areas of distress that initially bring on the experience of imbalances. These underlying imbalances can include everything from accident to attitude to illness. We have formulated a combination that we call the Master Blend. It is this combination that we feel enables us to do the most complete cleansing for the purpose of eradicating any and all predispositions to imbalance.

The methods of application are quite simple. Everyone should begin with the Master Blend combination, for an initial cleansing. This grouping of thirty-three stones works to clear the spirit, mind, and body of those factors that contributed to the initial imbalance. The hardest part about doing this therapy is remembering to do it faithfully for at least three weeks. Some individuals may require up to six weeks. After at least twenty-one days of consistent use, it is important that you reevaluate your condition. Some of your symptoms will have disappeared. As we discussed earlier, by the time we see evidence of imbalance in the physical body, the spirit and mind have already been affected and have rolled it down to the next level in an attempt to signal that something is wrong.

Adding Specific Combinations

After the cleansing period is over, you may then proceed with the specific combinations for the remaining symptoms. If medication is being used, those choices and amounts will change. In cases involving the use of synthesized chemicals, such as lithium or insulin, levels should be tested daily or at least with dramatically increased frequency, because as the body begins to heal, it will require less and less of prescribed medications. This applies to heart and blood pressure medications also. It can be very detrimental to take more of any medication than your body or condition requires. Your physician should be responsible for monitoring all prescribed medications. If your doctor is unwilling to work with you on this, I suggest you seek out one who will. After all, you are their employer.

Bear in mind also that much leeway exists in the three-week timetable guideline for the cleansing period. Some situations may require only brief assistance, of mere hours or days. This could be true of everything from irritating insect bites or rashes to the common cold or allergy attack. Then, on the other hand, depending upon the patient's age, duration of the illness, and its severity, the specific application may require many months. This could be true in the case of cataracts or in bringing one's vision back to 20-20.

The Master Blend

The complete Master Blend list, as described earlier, includes thirty-three stones and incorporates the seven physical cleansers as well. The Master Blend list is as follows:

Adamite	elimination of blame
Agate*	first aid, rescue, and guardian angel
Amazonite*	judgment
Amber**	memory/DNA structure; memory of wellness
Aventurine*	elimination of prejudice
Carnelian**	blood purifier for age 55 and older
Celestite	truth
Chrysocolla*	comprehension, education, matriarch, wisdom
Citrine	irritability and irritation
Clay**	detoxification of immune system
Coal	self-esteem
Covellite**	radiation toxicity
Diamond*	conscious harmony and balance
Dinosaur Bone	eliminates waste
Gold*	strength
Granite*	kindness and gentleness
Hematite**	blood purifier for ages 55 and under
Hemimorphite	transformation
Jade**	detoxification of emotional and spiritual residues
Jasper*	shield for positive outcomes
Kunzite	surrender
Lapis Lazuli	strengthening of spirit, transmitter
Moonstone ***(Labradorite)***	PMS-related syndromes and regular monthly upset
Onyx*	shielding from intense energy exchange
Opal*	elimination of fear or denial of divine calling

Petrified Wood*	stress
Pyrite**	air purification
Quartz Crystal	
Rose*	comfort and joy at times of sorrow over loss
Smoky**	water purification
Selenite	children's phobias and traumas
Sodalite*	celebration
Sugelite*	self-discipleship
Topaz*	changing negative energy to positive

* The Shield Stones

** The seven general cleansers (with hematite for those under age 55 and carnelian for those older than 55)

Shield Stones

Fifteen stones are known as shields. These stones are able to be worn or held literally 24 hours a day. Since they work as shields as opposed to detoxifying the system, they do not get toxic by way of use. They may be applied with any other combinations and are all found in the master blend. Some we suggest you make a part of your daily attire. One of the best we can recommend is petrified wood, for stress. Others include diamond and topaz. All these shields are recommended for use as preventative measures, especially after a regimen of Rock-Medicine has been applied for any preexistent conditions. Here is the complete list of the shield stones:

Agate	first, aid, rescue, and guardian angel
Amazonite	judgment
Aventurine	elimination of prejudice
Chrysocolla	comprehension, education, matriarch
Diamond	conscious harmony and balance
Gold	strength
Granite	kindness and gentleness
Jasper	shield for positive outcomes
Onyx	shielding from intense energy exchange
Opal	elimination of fear or denial of divine calling
Petrified Wood	stress
Quartz Crystal	
Rose	comfort and joy at times of sorrow over loss
Sodalite	celebration
Sugelite	self-discipleship
Topaz	changing negative energy to positive

The Seven Cleansers

As mentioned before, virtually all Rock-Medicine treatments begin with a combination that at least includes the seven physical or general cleansers. These are, along with their main healing attributes:

Amber	for memory/DNA structure/memory of wellness
Clay, Old *(over 200 yrs. old)*	for detoxification of immune system
Covellite	for removal of radiation toxicity
Hematite *(or* ***Carnelian*** *for those age 55 or older)*	for blood purification
Jade	detoxification of mental, physical, emotional, and spiritual residues
Pyrite	for air purification
Smoky Quartz	for water purification

The Seven General Cleansers form a basis for addressing many of the underlying *causes* of illness. The Master Blend of thirty-three stones goes on to more completely fulfill that purpose, and it includes all the seven cleansers!

Women's Hormonal Balance Formula

Lapis Lazuli	strengthening of spirit, transmitter
Opal	elimination of fear or denial of divine calling
Pearl	female reproductive system and nurturing

Men's Hormonal Balance Formula

Bornite	arrogance
Citrine	irritability and irritation
Ulexite	infidelity

The Stones

The Stones

It is most important that you use stones that are true representations of their mineral. At present, we are not encouraging the use of synthetic stones, as the evolutionary vibrations affecting this planet and all her kingdoms are not duplicated in simulated growth. The stones need not be of top quality. The size should be determined by your needs. If the instruments are going to be hand-held, obviously you do not want to choose pieces too large to hold comfortably together in one hand. Clear quartz used for essences needs to be of a size and shape that can fit easily into your water container and be retrieved. For the focus direct and blanket spreads, the size is limited only by your space and funds available, except for quartz in blanket spread and focus direct. A large stone does no more or less than a smaller piece. As long as there is one molecule of the mineral present, you will get the full chemical vibration of that element.

Seeking the most natural condition of stones is preferable. A rough, uncut piece is optimal; however, polished, tumbled, or carved stones work also. The only conditions of stones to avoid are any that have been altered by heat, dyes, or radiation. An example of this would be a blue topaz that has been irradiated to enhance its color. Another example is common black onyx, which is neither onyx nor naturally black. It is rather dyed agate.

Whenever you have a stone of multiple composite, such as azurite/malachite, it is the same as using both stones. Try to get clean, exclusive examples of rocks to use as tools. Whatever material is present will lend its influence to the mix. There may be occasions where you can chip away any unwanted material or matrix. It is imperative that there be no hidden veins of a secondary mineral which will change the overall composition of your healing equation. Certain matrices, such as granite and ironstone among others, are perfectly fine to use as they will not adversely affect the overall "sentence." Your best bet is to always seek the guidance of a qualified mineralogist, gemologist, or lapidary professional when purchasing your stones if you are unsure of the true identification or contents.

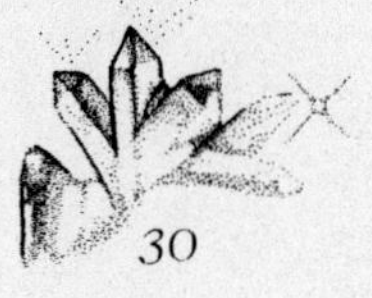

Abalone

Abalone is for domestic maturity.

This ocean offering of rainbows was once used by the Apache Indians during puberty ceremonies for adolescent girls. As the role of women in society has evolved, so too has the pertinence of domestic maturity as a nongender quality. Men as well as women are coming into a new awareness of taking a maternal outlook on life in their homes and communities. This quality of caretaking includes organizational skills as well as feeling at ease with the domestic chores and perceptions of cleanliness.

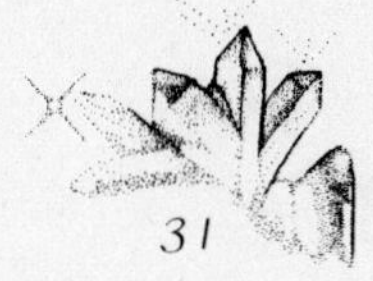

Cleanliness as applied to the physical mode is pretty self-explanatory. In terms of mental and spiritual cleanliness, it promotes comfort in one's abode. It is fitting yourself and your energies into the home-space in an orderly fashion. This facilitates a smooth-running household without becoming obsessive on the one hand or lackadaisical on the other. Bear in mind that the literal observance of domesticity is not the same as fidelity to the family unit. Domestic maturity is the comfort and ease with which one executes the responsibilities of a well-run home while keeping priorities in their proper order. Keeping a clean and orderly space for your body and possessions affords efficiency in physical undertakings, as does keeping the same degree of care for one's mental and spiritual homes.

Adamite

Adamite is for the elimination of blame.
Master Blend

Blame should not be confused with the concept of cause. When obstacles arise in one's life, it is important to see the causes in order to rise above them. However, from the beginning of man's fall from wellness, there has been an overwhelming tendency to lay blame in the course of dealing with one's problems. The first example we have of this syndrome is the story of the Garden of Eden. When asked whether or not he had eaten the fruit from the Tree of the Knowledge of Good and Evil, Adam didn't give a simple yes-or-no answer, but rather qualified his mistake as somehow being the fault of Eve, laying the blame on her. She, in turn, blamed the serpent. That same scenario is repeated in every walk of life right up to today, where we tend to blame others for undesirable political, economic, and environmental conditions. The bottom line should be, "Where do we stand at present, and where do we go from here?"

Rock-Medicine is here to deal with the vast array of imbalances afflicting this planet and its peoples. To be concerned with who and what is at fault for the present conditions would take as much time as all of history to date and would not repair things. Likewise, in dealing with the factors involved in interpersonal relationships and their failures, blaming is a waste of precious time and energy. There are only lessons to be learned from inappropriate actions by yourselves and others. As we enter the understanding of being one with all things, blame becomes a moot point of consideration. Growth is promoted by observation of potentials, for we learn just as much from mistakes as from successes. It is not possible to live long enough for every individual to make every mistake personally. The planet would never have survived. Instead, we can learn from the mistakes of others. In this light, it becomes easy to find love in your heart for that abusive parent, that lying lover, the baboonish politician, and the Hitlers of the world. Because their divine selves contracted to appear here in this existence to act as blatant examples of how *not* to be, we have been given the opportunity to act upon the lessons learned in life and to set standards to ensure our survival and growth. *Adamite is for those who are blaming themselves and/or others.*

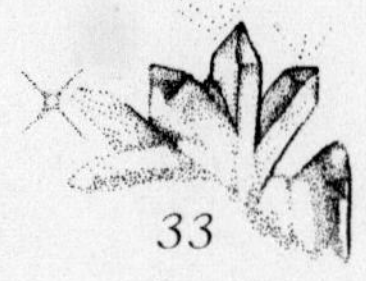

Agate

Agate is the guardian angel essence,
a first-aid and rescue remedy.
Master Blend / Shield Stone

"When in doubt—take your agate out!" Anytime you are less than happy, healthy, and high, we use agate until specifics are known or a more precise application is obtained.

Agate is a multicolored, frequently striped or banded chalcedony. The name "agate" came from an ancient river called Achates on the island of Sicily, a site once purported to have held large amounts of agate.

As first aid, agate should always be close at hand. It is nice that agate is very inexpensive and readily available. Any and all types of agate can be used; carnelian is the only agate that is used other than as an emergency tool. Agate is all-purpose first aid when held in one's hand. As with most of the stones, it can be used also as an essence.

In any given time of trauma, whether physical, emotional, or spiritual, agate will sustain your being and nurture to wellness everything from headache to heartache. Agate is the stone of choice for general assistance in any given situation. It is not by mere chance that so many "luck" items, like worry stones and worry beads, were made from this family of chalcedony.

Agate's vibrational influence is of value while one is working to overcome an addiction or habit. Agate is essential to the well-being of both young and old.

Alexandrite

Alexandrite is to assist men with their difficulties in adapting to the changes from a patriarchal to a matriarchal system.

This stone was named after Czar Alexander II. Alexandrite is a chrysoberyl, a rather rare stone, and very much needed at present. Due to its rarity, it is very expensive. It is important, as with all the stones, to make sure you have a genuine piece. My first essence was obtained by going into a fine jewelry shop. I took in a new jug of water with its top still sealed. The gentleman allowed me to put a one-carat alexandrite into the jug, which was later placed in the vault with all the other valuables at closing time. I picked up the gallon of alexandrite essence the next day!

This essence should be taken by all men, four times a day for seven to ten days minimum. It helps them become acclimated to the role of women in this new age and to the role of matriarchal energy in their own being. This influence is seen as an induction to enlightenment rather than therapy for a recurring malady. This application of help is not to be confused with or replaced by peridot for enlightened discernment, or petrified wood for emotional balance. This is a precise directive for the harmony and balance of strong, dominating male qualities and the feminine attributes of equality in service and contribution.

Some men are demonstrating many of the gentler aspects of the matriarchal strengths, such as parenting and homekeeping. These pioneer spirits will have a much easier transition than the proverbial "Archie Bunker" types.

Alexandrite aids in the change of states of awareness to a joyful acceptance of the value of nurturing and caring for each other, as in a brother being his brother's and sister's keeper.

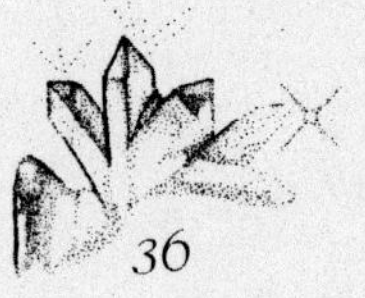

Amazonite

Amazonite is the stone that deals with judgment.
Master Blend / Shield Stone

The word *judgment* has gotten a bad rap. Judgment is something that we use every day. It is what helps us determine when it is safe to cross the street. We make value judgments all the time. What is not appropriate is to judge anyone too harshly. Amazonite removes attitudes of judgment regarding one's brethren's manner, custom, appearance, practices, and beliefs. Most important, Amazonite sets the value judgment center in balance while educating the conscious mind in utilizing good judgment.

Amazonite is to eliminate judgmental attitudes in us toward others, and in others toward us, and to foster good judgment. Amazonite came of age on August 16, 1987—the "Harmonic Convergence"— which was Judgment day, the day that the Age of Fire moved into the Age of Light. The laws of karma as we knew them were changed. This event was observed and shared around the world in thousands of different ways. From the meditating yogi on the mountaintop to the barfly celebrating humorously the "harmonica convention," all were involved. Such is the way of spirit, to have brought about these changes of ages in manners that would herald comfortably and soothingly the awakening of humankind to their Heaven, here on this Mother Earth.

According to many ancient doctrines, the Creator said He would pass by the earth and wanted to see at least 144,000 still faithful to the ways of the Spirit of Light. On that day of Harmonic Convergence, August 16, 1987, we showed closer to 144 million of us looking for the Love Light! The vote, or judgment, of the peoples was toward Peace. Of course, we outdid ourselves. How could we not, since we are all part and one with this great creation? By the gifts and tools of enlightenment, our judgment went in full favor of Harmony, Peace, and Love. We've already won. We are safe, saved, and secure.

In our well-recorded history, we have the guarantee of this new age. Humankind's abilities have taken hatred and lies to a state of art. Nazi Germany and the threat of nuclear annihilation are two good examples. When we've applied our new knowledge of the mineral kingdom to the daily task of wellness for ourselves and our environment, we will live in a state of readiness to experience the Divine Presence. In a state of well-being, it is guaranteed that you will not find any two or three together in any name but Love.

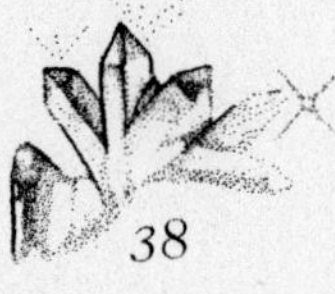

Amazonite begins a precious course of healing for us all. Rock-Medicine is a comprehensive modality for vibrational balancing of the physical, mental, and spiritual bodies. Amazonite is particularly well-sistered with aventurine, which is the stone used to counter prejudice.

Amber

Amber is the memory stone, and for proper DNA structure.
Master Blend / General Cleanser

Amber is a fossilized form of pine resin. It is one of the oldest crystal formations on the planet. Amber is essential to any application of Rock-Medicine, as it carries the memory to the area afflicted of what that area's proper state of wellness is. This quality would be especially applicable in extreme cases such as multiple sclerosis, Alzheimer's, and muscular dystrophy. Amber is one of the stones indicated to use for ALL physical maladies.

Amber uses your own DNA to lock on to a previously well state. Because the DNA holds the patterns of every one of your ancestors, if you are born with an imbalance, amber will search back as many generations as necessary to find a healthy strand to lock on to and use as its guide.

Being the memory stone, it is quite literally applied to anyone whose memory is ailing. Effective uses may be in recalling specific events in this lifetime, or for past life recall. Amber is not, however, the stone for past-life regression. That stone is talc.

Just as a single cell of our body carries the full equation of our being, so it is with the stones themselves. One small chip or fragment of any stone is just as effective as a huge boulder-sized one. Each one of the stone's cells carries the full vibration of that stone's influence.

As long as it is a true representative of its particular mineral family, your Rock-Medicine instruments can be of any size. It is more a question of practicality as to what rocks each household acquires.

Memory of wellness applies as equally to the physical broken leg as it does to the mental and spiritual attributes that allowed the break in the first place. Researching ancient Egypt, we find the presence of great amounts of amber. The Atlanteans took stone-healing principles to Egypt, among other places. Also, they brought the Egyptians the higher-level techniques of vibrational power-wielding, such as telekinesis and levitation. Isis is one of the most well-remembered Atlanteans. Her job was—and still is—to teach humankind to heal.

Inspiration is the conscious memory of the future.

Amethyst

Amethyst is for cell division and for alcohol detoxification.

Amethyst comes from the Greeks, meaning literally "not intoxicated" or not toxic. This has been and remains an influence of this stone's vibration. When drinking alcohol, if an amethyst is placed in the glass or bottle, its energy negates the physically toxic poisons. This means you get the same altered state of consciousness, but no headache, nausea, or hangover, no matter how much is drunk. Either a real amethyst gem or quartz may be used here. However, this use comes with a grave area of caution: If one has a problem with alcoholism, such as blackouts, rages, depression, or dependency, this is an addiction and must first be addressed as such.

The sages of old used wine for altering their states of consciousness, just as our culture uses drugs or various exercises to alter ours and evoke an expanded state of mind to create new ideas. The danger that alcohol poses is its toxicity. Anything used to excess is toxic. (Don't worry, though, there is no such thing as an excess of love, as nothing exceeds it!)

Amethyst can be used as an application for cell mitosis (or cell division), or anywhere there is a disruption of the cell structure. Whether it be a broken bone, tumorous growth, tissue breakdown, or even acne, amethyst catalyzes cell movement. Amethyst should never be used alone, for it is as a soldier with blinders on to all but its job to cause cells to divide, and it makes no distinction on its own between well and ill cell structures. It receives its direction from the stones you add to it. Amethyst should not be worn alone, as its nature will serve to cause more severe results at times of burns, cuts, and all other types of injury.

In a situation such as cancer, where the action of the illness is mutating cells, amethyst alone would serve to perpetuate the mutation. Using calcite, which is anticancer, with the amethyst changes the polarity of its influence, and it then addresses the cancer. Any time you need to elicit the actual changing of cell structure in the body, amethyst is used. This includes all physical applications. Amethyst is not in the Master Blend, so that the spirit and mind may be initially cleansed before beginning work on the physical body. Because of its ability to speed up the action of cell division, it is an excellent tool for use in infertility.

Amethyst can be administered to one who is intoxicated by alcohol, for detoxification, when combined with jade, smoky quartz, hematite, and lepidolite. The benefits of this stone are limitless. Amethyst quartz in its rough mineral state is inexpensive and readily available, although gem quality amethyst works equally well.

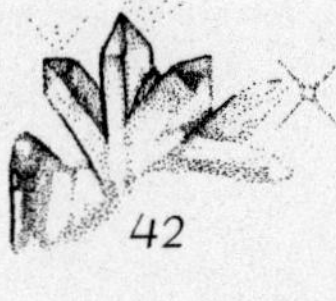

All minerals work to their highest potential when in their most natural state.

Apatite

Apatite is for proper metabolizing of nutrients.

This stone is a very good example of how simple this work truly is. This crystal is named for just about what it addresses. Any weight or food allergy problem should be treated with apatite, as this stone balances the body's metabolism. While allergies are the result of improper metabolization, weight problems rarely are. Eating disorders take many different forms. Food is used for comfort, for boredom, even for protection. There are many people who consciously or unconsciously gain weight to prevent relationships, for example. The self-destructive behavior of bulimia represents many different problems going on within the spectrum of self-image and self-love but ultimately results in a damaged metabolism. Once someone is at a critical stage with their weight, their body's ability to metabolize food has been compromised. All weight imbalance situations require metabolism balancing, whether it be for obesity or anorexia. Both these illnesses are emotionally based diseases with dramatic physical symptoms. The symptoms have subsequent residuals, such as the metabolism going awry.

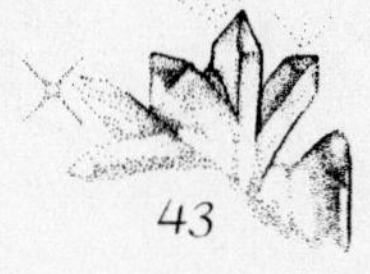

Proper digestion of food is typified by the adage, "You are what you eat." Just think a moment about the mental and spiritual correlation to the obvious physical meaning.

Our beautiful mother Earth has provided us with a vast array of nutritional staples. It is a common fallacy among the metaphysical community that any member of the animal kingdom is off limits as a foodstuff. This is as ludicrous a belief as the assumption that the mineral kingdom does not having consciously controlled powers of cause and effect. All that exists is made up of light energy. This includes all elements of the animal, vegetable, and mineral kingdoms. Being of the same light energy, yet vibrating at individual rates of speed to produce individuality, all things, therefore, carry within themselves the full spectrum of light color bands. This correlation between the various kingdoms of life forms is what enables us to utilize herbs, for example, to address a malady.

Today, toxic levels of impurities, both from airborne pollutants and radiation, as well as soil and water pollutants, are contaminating our entire environment. It is virtually impossible to obtain untainted food or herbs unless they are raised hydroponically with purified water in a sterile atmosphere. This is not by any means cost-effective or practical at present. Nor is it necessary, since we now have these age-old instruments to help us clean up ourselves *and* the environment. You cannot treat something toxic with something toxic and get anything other than something equally toxic.

All that we take in, on every level, becomes some part of our being. Whenever you ingest or partake of anything, you are making its qualities one with yours. This applies also to the consumption of meat products. In the case of venison, the deer is a gentle and beautifully spirited animal. In offering thanks before a meal, we consciously acknowledge the sacrifice of what we are about to receive. Then we can accept with celebration and appreciation all that has been provided to meet our every need.

Because we are all light energy, correlating bands of intensity match each of the mineral, vegetable, and animal kingdoms. When we find the "matches," so to speak, we can use the influence of one in order to tune or balance another. This is the principle upon which all things work to elicit harmony or well-being.

Aquamarine

Aquamarine indicates the mouth.

The name "aquamarine" is derived from Latin and means "water of the sea."

The application of this stone in combination with others signifies that the area of illness is located in the mouth. Combining aquamarine with coral and the seven cleansers specifies treatment of the teeth and jawbone. Aquamarine with rhodochrosite addresses the gums and other tissue in the mouth. It will serve to eliminate inflammation, infection, and pain, as well as help with more serious conditions until a dental practitioner can be seen. An essence can be applied topically, directly on the area, such as in the case of a teething baby. Amethyst will be used in all physical applications, as here with aquamarine, as it promotes cell division which is necessary to elicit tangible physical change.

These instruments are not meant to replace conventional medical practices as a whole. Rather, they work in conjunction with them. However, certain forms of chemical and physical therapy have toxic residuals and side effects. These may be replaced by Rock-Medicine. Although there are several safeguards and cautions for using Rock-Medicine, they are standardized and easily observable.

A broken tooth, injured gum, or root decay are problems that require some physical assistance from qualified professionals. Just as when one breaks a leg, obvious action must be taken as well as applying the appropriate stones, such as for pain, cell mitosis, and emotional balance.

Aragonite

Aragonite is for community unity.

Aragonite is a crystallized deposit of hot spring calcium carbonate. It is for the relationship between the masses, between neighbors, friends, and acquaintances. This stone is for unity and all that it represents. It is especially suited for disputes between friends, business associates, fellow students or workers, club or church members, or any time that a group or community formed as a body finds itself amid dissent. (For the application of this same kindredship between family members, use ulexite. Aragonite may be added also). This mineral is best known for its appearance as stalactites and stalagmites in Carlsbad Caverns and other underground caves.

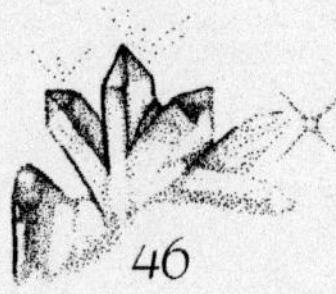

A less well-known occurrence of major proportions is in Nevada at the Pyramid Lake Paiute Indian Reservation. The Pyramid Lake area is made up of vast deposits of this mineral, which is also called tufa. It is no wonder then that this was the site of a musical event held specifically to send out a vibrational spiral of unity and healing. This event was called "Ranch Rock." One of the miraculous results of that show was to preserve the rights of the Paiutes to their water. The outcome of that show's energy was the defeat of a cruel move on the part of greedy politicians and land barons. Some of the earliest prophecies concerning the rainbow tribe (a united humankind) have come out of the Paiute teachings. On September 7, 1986, the gathering there joined in dance, prayer, and song. It became the germination process of a collective of seeds carried among many hearts. We are starting to see the possibilities of unity, and that is what we must see in order to create it.

This stone represents an intensifying of a world unity. Nowhere more than in the concept of unity do we see the potential for the success of a vibratory spiral of positive energy. The Yin must always be, and so must the Yang. Fortunately for us, the interplay of the karmic equation enables us to experience negativity and then arrive at an attainable point of being "done" with manifesting its presence. Only after this occurrence does the guarantee ensuring a bright future come into effect regarding our lessons from the past.

Aragonite unites our spirits individually and collectively, as well as our mental capacities and physical interactions. (The only exception is one's uniting with the higher consciousness, which is the work of diamond.)

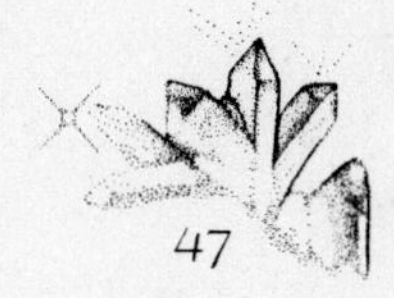

Aventurine

Aventurine is to eliminate prejudice of any kind.
Master Blend / Shield Stone

This glossy green stone was named in the seventeenth century after a green Italian glass known as *aventura,* which it resembled. As mentioned earlier, this stone is a companion stone to amazonite, which is for judgment. Aventurine addresses all forms of prejudice, including the obvious aspects such as race, creed, and religion, and also in countering prejudicial attitudes regarding sexual preferences, attire, mannerisms, handicaps, and behaviors.

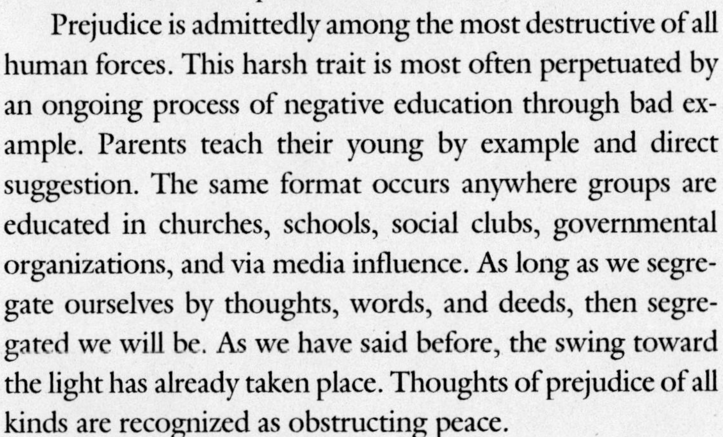

Prejudice is admittedly among the most destructive of all human forces. This harsh trait is most often perpetuated by an ongoing process of negative education through bad example. Parents teach their young by example and direct suggestion. The same format occurs anywhere groups are educated in churches, schools, social clubs, governmental organizations, and via media influence. As long as we segregate ourselves by thoughts, words, and deeds, then segregated we will be. As we have said before, the swing toward the light has already taken place. Thoughts of prejudice of all kinds are recognized as obstructing peace.

Aventurine may be used for your own feelings of prejudice, as well as to disrupt incoming energies that would methodically participate in prejudicial thoughts, words, or deeds. It gives radical strength to all antiprejudice activity. We must be very careful about our own thoughts and inner state, as these tones resonate higher as they emanate from us and around us. Our job is to shed light by example. It has oft been said, "The wise man has the power." Wisdom is the discretion and tact with which we convert knowledge into action and pursue that which nurtures and perpetuates the positive growth of all creation.

Changes of this type can occur only as they do in nature, that is, in a flow of adaptation within the evolutionary process and in a kind and considerate manner toward our oneness. This state also requires enlightenment or conscious awakening of the spirit as a catalyst.

Azurite

Azurite is to promote "self-healing" and to enhance the usage of time spent in the "dream state."

This brilliant blue stone gets its name from its azure blue color. When you see a particularly well-crystallized example, it is almost possible to see the universe in its glimmer. Azurite is a most precious stone, in that it facilitates the self-healing process, expressly in those times when we do not have a diagnosis. This is invaluable when the nature of so many maladies eludes us at present. Using its vibration, the stone sends the unconscious mind on a seeking mission, as it were. It travels throughout the body, mind, and spirit and combines the input with its own information.

You may be asking then, "Why not just use azurite for every ailment?" Azurite has been provided in the event that the truth about an infirmity remains unknown. It is applied *because* you do not have a diagnosis, and it also hastens the discovery of one. Obviously, you would then switch to a combination of stones to elicit much more expedient healing that specifically and precisely tunes the correlating band of vibration inherent to the affected area.

When azurite is used to work in conjunction with the dream state, the application is that the stone be held on the forehead or third eye for 10 to 15 minutes right before going to sleep. Do not secure it there and try to sleep, for it creates a disquieting saturation when overapplied. This method of obtaining first-person presence in your sleep state is one that allows you to consciously continue your self-improvement process on the mental and spiritual levels while the physical body is resting. Working with dreams is progressive: you first begin to remember your dreams more vividly. You then progress to understanding your dreams, interacting with your dreams, and finally traveling and interacting with others in the dream state. Many personal and global conflicts can be resolved thereby, as so many fewer inhibitions exist in this state.

It is advisable to take a break from our daily routine at least once a week. This is the day you choose to take as your Sabbath. A day of reflection is essential to the harmony of everyone's week. It is absurd to think that the Creator had need of rest/relaxation and we do not, especially now, at this birthing and beginning of a new world.

Azurite is quite often found growing jointly with malachite. You must make sure that there is no malachite on the azurite at all. Azurite is one tool unto itself, malachite is another, and the combination of the two form yet a third. The combination rock, azurite/malachite, is for paranoid schizophrenia, a condition that at present has reached epidemic proportions worldwide.

Azurite/Malachite

Azurite/Malachite is for paranoid schizophrenia.

Representing extreme basic fear, paranoid schizophrenia is the most prominent epidemic planetwide. This is not surprising when we learn that radiation toxicity affects human beings in the thyroid gland. The thyroid gland is the seat of both inspiration and anxiety. When thyroid toxicity goes untreated by covellite, the resulting illness is the condition known as paranoia and paranoid schizophrenia. At this advanced stage, covellite alone is not effective, and thus the introduction of azurite/malachite. Either a single stone containing both elements or two stones, one of each type, may be used.

The application needed may be anywhere from 10 days to 8 weeks, depending upon the severity of the condition.

When we consider the individual influences of these two elements, which almost exclusively grow together, we can see how they combine their qualities for use here. Azurite promotes self-healing. Without the ability of the mind to perceive a state of wellness, azurite works to independently reorganize the thought processes for the return of mental clarity. Malachite brings focus of vision. As the azurite balances one's perception of reality, the malachite centers the mind's eye on a conscious focus of that reality and thus enables one to return to mental stability.

In order to prevent the return of the advanced toxicity, a continued application of covellite is required until such time as the radiation levels in the environment return to a natural and safe level. Covellite is needed by all things living at this point in time, and azurite/malachite is also highly advisable for use as a preventive measure by all humans.

The ability to manifest creative desire is the single most valuable prerequisite for the promotion of a healthy existence on this planet.

Barite

Barite is for fungi. Moldavite is for molds.

The use of both of these together is advised when treating such situations as ringworm, candida, yeast infections, and the like.

Remember to include all pertinent information while forming your Rock-Medicine sentence. First, begin with the Master Blend. The barite and moldavite will be directed to the involved area(s). In the example of ringworm, you would then go on to include rhodochrosite, which says, "epidermal tissue." Add amethyst for the motion of cell division, and for this single condition you have a complete prescription. Barite and moldavite are good for allergies and sensitivities to mold.

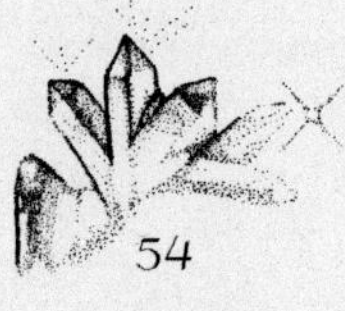

Beryl

Beryl is to awaken the psyche to its skills and education (i.e.: psychic awareness, abilities such as clairvoyance, telepathy, foresight, traveling out of body, and so on).

Beryl is any member of the "precious beryl" family not being aquamarine or emerald. The green and yellow forms are most frequently seen around local lapidary shops. Red is rare, but all beryls work equally well, no matter what the color. One of the primary occurrences at the Harmonic Convergence was that the minerals' evolution of vibration converged with each other. As a result, jade is jade is jade, no matter the color; agate is agate is agate, no matter the type. So it is with all mineral families. There are a few variations on this theme, but they are well indicated in this text.

Good judgment is called for when working with stones of a higher vibration. A state of well-being is necessary for any growth process. Always address the necessary and immediate relief from illness, whether it be poor vision, allergies, or any physical imbalance, before proceeding with your application. Although we already envision the true potentials before us, as is typified in new age art and music, we must follow a strategic guideline and design. Out-of-body experiences are preliminary exercises predisposed to make the ways of teleportation, astral travel, time travel, and the like, obtainable. Before such an advanced culture can exist, however, a lot of work, cooperation, and organization is necessary to help the higher consciousness with the practical and technological, as well as medical, needs of this particular plane of existence. You must begin at the beginning. Learning to stand precedes learning to walk, which in turn precedes learning to run.

Bloodstone

Bloodstone is for the HIV virus.

AIDS is not a "sexual" disease. Having AIDS means having the HIV virus in the bloodstream and one's T cell count below 200. This attack upon the immune system and the resultant breakdown of natural defenses opens one up or makes one vulnerable to virtually all invasive infections. Bloodstone is specifically for the elimination of the HIV presence from the bloodstream at the pre-AIDS stage. As with other diseases treated by Rock-Medicine, this application is to heal the condition present and not to merely maintain or sustain the present level of a given illness.

The Master Blend combined with heliotrope and amethyst are for the elimination of the HIV virus. If other conditions are present, such as brain infection and/or lesions, tumors, abrasions, etc., these must all be treated with additional combinations of stones per their specific nature. The use of the combination of stones for AIDS can also be used preventively by those close to and/or working with AIDS victims.

Of course, as with all illnesses, it is most beneficial to treat the afflicted with the utmost love, kindness, and regard for their dignity. Nowhere more than in dealing with this deadly disease has this issue come forth. We should always remember this lesson in caring for that which is not well of body, mind, or spirit.

Bornite

Bornite is the stone to overcome arrogance.
Male Hormonal Balance

Bornite is one of three stones which combine for male hormone balance. It is a metallic, rainbow-lustered rock. Its slang name is "peacock ore." It is the first stone we come to that is a hormone balancer for men. In combination with ulexite and citrine, it brings the full male hormonal fabric into balance on the physical, emotional, and spiritual bodies. All individuals have male and female hormones. However, women never require this combination for male hormone balance, though one or two of the three individual stones will certainly apply at times. No matter what gender you consider yourself, it is your biological chromosomal origin that determines your use of the male triad vs. the female triad.

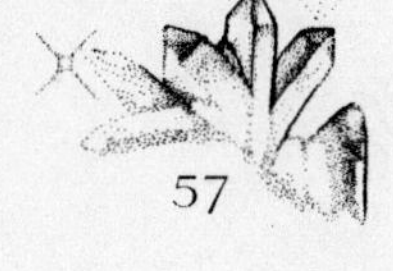

This glittery stone does away with unnecessary and even dangerous trappings. Self-righteous attitudes, arrogance, pride—these are qualities that contributed to the unbalanced social system known as "patriarchal."

The opposition of patriarchal to matriarchal is not necessarily consistent with male-female relationships, but rather the relativity of an individual's perception of the best of both those qualities within themselves. For example, many men exhibit matriarchal wisdom and gentility, while many women are demonstratively patriarchal in their attitudes of division and control. We see the contrast between the beauty of the divine father aspect and the potential ugliness when this aspect is out of balance, which creates thoughts, words, and deeds that are overbearing as opposed to bearing up or being supportive of one another, controlling and commanding of others rather than developing one's own self-discipline. The masculine-patriarchal leadership forces that have been out of balance for so long on Earth are resulting in the death and destruction of the human spirit.

Rising out of that cycle, to balance it, is its natural counterpart, or polar opposite, which is the feminine-matriarchal tendency toward home-keeping and fostering young. This quality is a partner to fidelity. Fidelity means faithful, loyal, and true. This concept is demonstrated in the fable of the ugly duckling who survived due to the care of the mother. This degree of care needs to be undertaken by men as well as women in our present society and is promoted by the use of bornite.

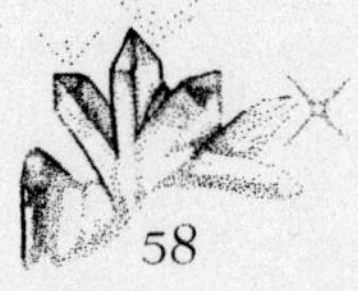

Calcite

Calcite is for cancer.
(There are some specifics pertaining to color.)

Cancer is a disease of attitude. Calcite may be used as a preventive measure where one's attitude indicates a predisposition to manifesting this disease. Those who attempt to suppress anger create blockages that fester and grow malignantly. Anger arises due to a person's perception that their freedom has been denied, as when a wild animal loses its spirit as a result of being caged. The direct use of calcite on cancer is as follows:

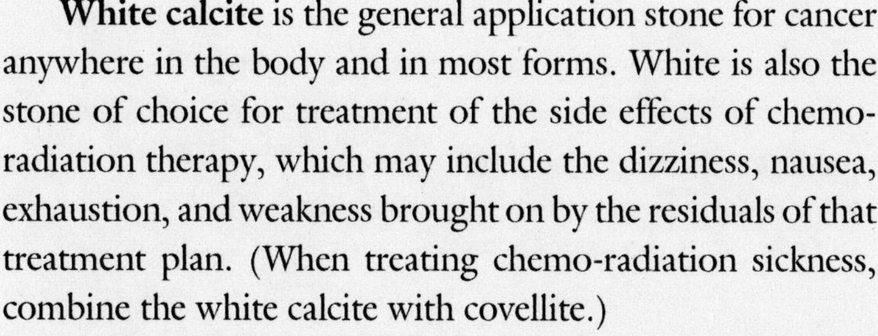

White calcite is the general application stone for cancer anywhere in the body and in most forms. White is also the stone of choice for treatment of the side effects of chemo-radiation therapy, which may include the dizziness, nausea, exhaustion, and weakness brought on by the residuals of that treatment plan. (When treating chemo-radiation sickness, combine the white calcite with covellite.)

The condition of cancer is a stranger to no area of our body. Therefore, as you treat the causes in general, you need to pay particular attention to the information pertaining to the specific body part(s) involved (i.e., Herkimer diamond's effect on the throat, larynx, vocal chords, and voice box).

Pink calcite is most specifically for leukemia. It is applicable to sickle-cell anemia also. Ultimately we shall locate a pink calcite chamber on the planet wherein many similarly evolved blood disorders will be speedily cured. Remember that leukemia is a form of cancer, and the underlying emotional causes need to be evaluated and addressed.

Yellow calcite is for cancers in the kidneys, liver, pancreas, bladder, uterus, and vagina. When there is an affliction in any one of these areas that is not cancer, then the yellow calcite can serve as the stone that directs the help of other specific stones to this area. The same applies to green calcite and blue calcite, for their respective domains.

Green calcite is applied when the areas afflicted are in the spleen, colon, intestines, or digestive tract.

Blue calcite is indicated for use where the lymph or glandular system is infected with the cancer.

Calcite will always be used for cancers. This includes external as well as internal eruptions. Again note that the use of the various colored calcites is not exclusive to cancerous conditions but may be incorporated into combinations where the calcite is indicating the area of affliction.

Carnelian

Carnelian is for use by those over 55 as a blood purifier, strengthener, and vitality enhancer.
Master Blend / General Cleanser

It is named for its color, which resembles that of a type of cherry known as the Kornel. The specification regarding age is due to the difference between the generations. The blood evolution of one generation resonates at a slightly different rate than the hemostructure of the next generation. (The stone of choice for blood purification by the generation under 55 is hematite.) Therefore, the carnelian would replace or, if in doubt, would be added to the hematite in the Master Blend grouping. The application can be either by hand or by essence, in a four-times-a-day standard application.

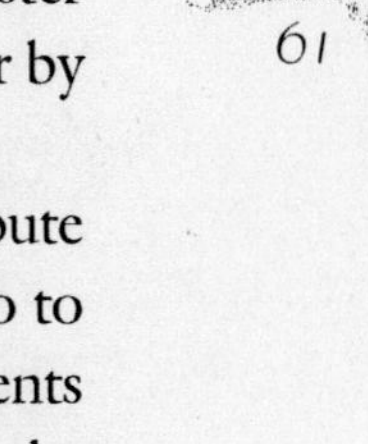

As it is the function of the heart to process and distribute the blood throughout one's system, it is always wise also to treat the heart with cinnabar, especially in geriatric patients who are having blood disorders. (See **Cinnabar**.) Since the three bodies (physical, mental, and spiritual) are joined, enhancing the performance of the blood itself, and all such flows, can be addressed by these stones.

Garnet, too, may be indicated for use as it controls blood pressure. (See **Garnet**.)

Celestite

Celestite is for Truth.
Master Blend

All perceivable aspects regarding Truth are most expeditiously addressed with celestite, whether it be the truth about a situation, one's ability to handle a given truth, or even the fortitude to elicit the truth. Celestite's presence serves as a reminder of the importance of Truth to all existence, especially considering the fact that we progress by way of adaptation and, if unnatural or untrue energies do too much damage, we could lose irretrievable opportunities.

No situation exists in which lies are better than the truth, but there is a certain amount of truth that is painful. This is sometimes unavoidable. An abuse or incorrect use of the truth occurs when the intended result is to hurt another.

Celestite is better suited for states of denial than any other stone, especially regarding addictions and attitude or behavior problems. The sociopath denies his relationship to the world around him and would therefore also be treated with celestite. (If the source of his pathological behavior is found to be organic, add lepidolite for brain chemical balance.)

An ancient legend typifies for us the value of the naked truth. Truth and Falsehood once went bathing. When they came out of the water, Falsehood ran ahead, dressed herself in Truth's clothing and ran away. Truth, unwilling to appear in Falsehood's clothing, went "naked." It is no wonder the most heinous of personages conceptualized by humankind is the satanic "Father of Lies." All evil is represented by the absence of the Light of Truth.

Knowing the "absolute truth" of our existence better equips us to take more total control of ourselves in our environment and relationships. Chronic and habitual lying and/or the presence of delusion are an indication for the use of this stone. (This does not include artificially induced states of delusion.) Lies are love's polar opposite. Without the benefit of Truth as your grounding, it is impossible to evolve beyond the Earthbound state of being.

Chalcedony

Chalcedony is a shield system.

The chalcedony family is a large group that includes the agates, chrysoprase, heliotrope, fossilized wood, jasper, carnelian, onyx, and sand. (See the individual stones for descriptions.)

As you continue through this text, note the variations on the precise applications of like or related minerals. We shall continue to describe the individual stones in our overall alphabetical presentation; just bear in mind that this is a mineral family with many similarities in appearance, thus the categorical reference to them as chalcedony for their structural identification. Different stones provide different types of protection or shielding. Some of these differences are very subtle, as in the effects of jasper and onyx.

Chrysocolla

Chrysocolla is for the comprehension, recall, retention, and application of one's education. It is the matriarchal stone. Master Blend / Shield Stone

This vibrant, blue-green beauty is a queen among stones. She is the manifestation of wisdom. Education is a result of being conscious. We are all educating ourselves, in every working sense, throughout our lives. Once it was a respected thing to have an *alma mater.* Indicating a college education, this term was coined from the Latin phrase that means, literally, "nursing," or nourishing mother. The implication is that a nourished or nurtured mind is fundamental to survival, and even more so to growth.

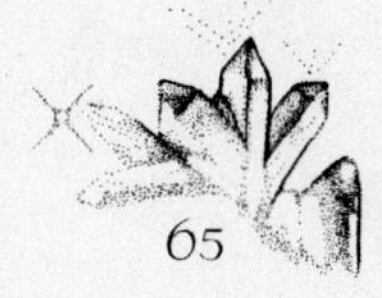

The earliest thought-processing periods in one's life are the most important, by virtue of their duration throughout our lives. It is well known that all of our primary, or "gut level," responses to external influences are in place by the age of five. The longer information is stored in the brain, the more its virtues are understood by the conscious and subconscious repetition of those resources. The matriarchal quality causes the mother to place infinite value on the baby. The younger the baby, the more pure and vulnerable it is. So too, we must nurture this new enlightened state of being into growth, health, and expansion.

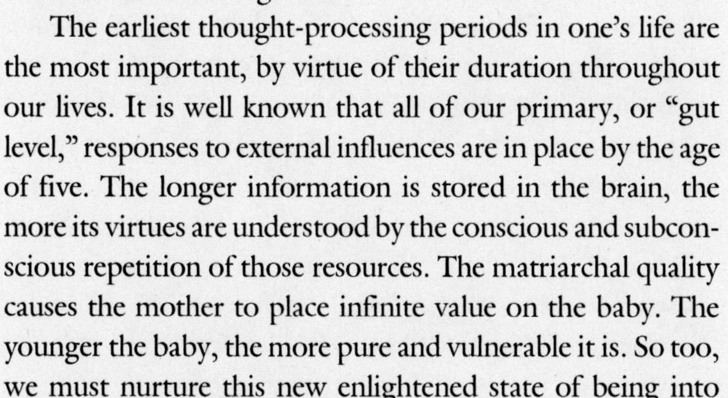

We are at a point in time that calls upon all of us to take conscious responsibility for our oneness. If there is to be any future for humankind, it includes compassion toward one another. Compassion is not a passive quality but rather an active one. We may not be able to envision the saving of the world from its misery as a whole, but this will be the result of us all taking action to improve the lives of those whom life puts in our path. This may mean offering food, clothing, or shelter to someone in need. It may merely be to extend simple kindness in the form of a smile. It is important to remember that when a person is at their least lovable, they most need our hugs and love. Incorporating this mindset daily in our personal lives will impact the global situation.

Chrysocolla is, therefore, ideal for one's academic pursuits as well as one's spiritual, moral, and character development. Use chrysocolla by holding the stone in the appropriate hand while studying, reading, attending lecture/class, or during tests. This applies to any type of formal learning situation, whether it be on the physical, mental, or spiritual level. Being a shield stone, there is no time limit for its application in a given sitting. It can also be worn as an amulet, never needing to be removed.

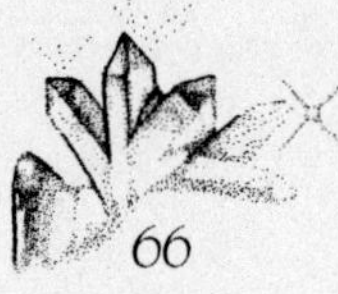

Actually, both the subconscious and the conscious minds are conscious. It is their interaction with the whole that determines the level of quality and success of our education in consciousness. Higher consciousness results in demonstrating wisdom. In this world of third-dimensional limitation, we have received both the tools and the education to improve the quality of all existence on a conscious level. These gifts were wrought from our own world's collective conscious and subconscious creative knowledge so that we can manifest our destiny—to be enlightened.

Using chrysocolla for higher studies works particularly well when it's joined with silver, as this combination causes a vortex of energy to be directed at the highest chakra point, at the apex of the electrical field which surrounds your being. This might be described as the point located above your crown chakra. The Harmonic Convergence enabled us to be aware of every cell in our body as the chakra or energy entry and exit point that it is. This awakening provides us with the fundamental keen awareness that is required for self-control, subsequent spiritual progress, and the realization of universal Love.

Where knowledge or Truth is present with self-discipline or proper education, there in their midst is unconditional Love.

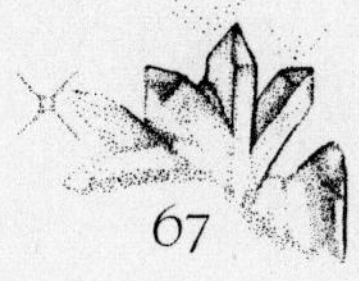

Chrysoprase

Chrysoprase is for pain.

This translucent, apple- to bluish-green stone is much needed for its influences in addressing the despair of pain. Pain weighs heavily on the mind, body, and soul. It always takes an obvious toll on one's life.

When addressing physical pain from injury, surgery, or strain, the most effective application is to hold it in the appropriate hand as needed. Now if the pain has served its purpose in indicating to the being the presence of damage, then you do well to go ahead and treat the pain. If, however, the cause of the pain has not been determined, then the pain is still a needed source to draw information from in order to form a diagnosis. A clear diagnosis is always necessary before the elimination of one's pain is appropriate. Chrysoprase is the best known treatment for relief from pain, which in turn makes one more receptive to treatment of the source. Chrysoprase puts a barrier between you and the pain's discomfort.

Emotional pain parallels the physical and spiritual levels. The height of pain may be seen on the face of the Creator and can only be likened unto the most agonizing of losses over a loved one. Take the extreme you've known in any given moment of true breakage of the heart or spirit and know that HE has felt this, and more, since we have been away from each other for these millennia. The divine presence is as ready as we are for heaven on earth.

The most assured way to do away with pain and sickness is to decide to do so! That is the act of faith. Proclaiming so by way of example and opinion represents an act of commitment. Semantics has never come into play more than in these times of mass communication. The term "decide" comes from Latin and means "cutting away": *decidere*—arriving at a decision by eliminating all but one possibility, by cutting away all that is unneeded or excess. In this time of awakening to the presence of a higher consciousness, let's not be so concerned as to which of His infinite names we call Her, but that we all do call upon the availability of the benefits of unconditional Love in our individual and united daily lives. We were conceived of Love and Light, and our potential for growth flourishes nowhere better than under those conditions which Love promotes. This same Love, a conscious thought, placed a healing vibrational instrument inside solid rock, safe and within hand's-reach to await its coming of age. We always have been safe in the rock of ages. That the desire for Love to lead us is again humankind's desire is well represented by the way this world is making known its desire for peace. It has evolved to conscious action and has won us the opportunity to choose eternity. Chrysoprase allows us to choose to be without pain.

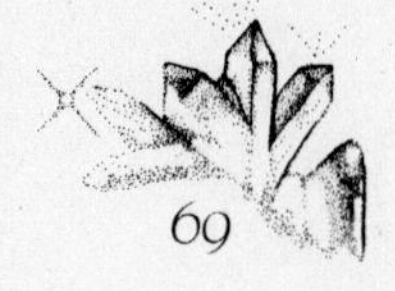

For cases of long-term, chronic physical pain, you would do well to use an essence and saturation level to elicit complete relief over a period of some three to four weeks, bearing in mind always that whenever a standard of application does not work, you are using the wrong one. Reevaluate if necessary.

Cinnabar

Cinnabar is for the strength of the heart muscle and its valve function.

This stone directs healing to the physical muscle, the heart. It is useful in all cases of heart disease. Some heart troubles may include angina, murmurs, holes, obstructions, and valve damage.

Cinnabar is extremely mercury-toxic. Mercury poisoning could result if it is handled too much or if it were to be ingested. So, obviously, you would not make an essence out of it or hand-hold it. The safe way to use your cinnabar is to keep a clear quartz crystal stored with it, thus setting the crystal to "be" cinnabar. The quartz, once wiped thoroughly clean of any cinnabar dust, may be used safely in either hand-held or essence form.

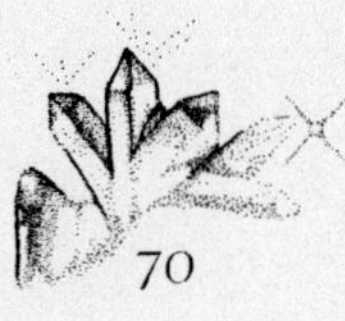

Cinnabar no doubt got its name from its beautifully rich cinnamon color. This ancient Chinese favorite is not easily come by, as it is rare, toxic, and expensive. Our hearts carry the life force in all definitions of that term. Man has seen through the lion's den of hell by virtue of his conviction of heart. The heart has been the keeper of the lovelight and its progress. The ancient Greeks coined the term "to learn something by heart," based upon their belief that the heart was the seat of thought. As we see by the timely reinstatement of the mineral kingdom's vibrational tools, even a stone—especially a stone—has conscious placement in service of value. So take heart; all hearts of stone can be softened with the one called Cinnabar.

The conditions existing in the emotional and spiritual aspects of the heart coincide. However, romantic interaction is an exception to the use of this stone for the heart. For romantic issues, see the guidelines for ruby. At the harmonic convergence, the seat of thought moved, evolved, and transitioned upward, to relocate itself in its new anatomical position atop the aura. Do not confuse the function of the heart in venting a portion of the grief process with its capacity for acting as the agent of awareness. In the first function, that of the fundamental acknowledgment of a loss, the ensuing distresses are healed with rose quartz.

The heart also harbors trust. It guides the energy known as the truth chord. That's the thing that gives us goose bumps of affirmation! To consciously confirm our understandings, we apply cinnabar. Note that heart damage and scar tissue, or their equivalents, resonate as a presence in each of the three bodies. Think carefully before causing damage to another's heart, as each time you do so, you take an element of wholeness from yourself. Cinnabar is also invaluable for pre- and post-heart surgery.

Citrine

Citrine is for irritability.
Master Blend / Men's Hormonal Balance

Citrine is one of the triad for male hormone balance and is also for itching. We have yet to know all about this stone. The golden sunny yellow of this stone serves to remind us of its virtues. Citrine combines with ulexite and bornite for bringing harmony to the male hormone system. As stated with bornite, women had best never use the combination of the three. They will, however, find use of the individual stones in certain applications. Citrine alone relieves irritability, manic behavior, and the inability to organize and tend to our relationship with our environment. It is for energies that are scattered and working at odds with each other, and for counterproductive or self-destructive tendencies. These are all strong patriarchal characteristics.

We find that citrine is particularly soothing to skin irritations, but only to the itch itself, not the physical presence of rash or outbreak. Since both sensory manifestations are often simultaneous, one may welcome relief from the itch while working to diagnose the condition. Citrine is applicable in this way for allergic reactions, fungi, insect bites, and organic rashes like poison ivy and poison oak, just to name a few. Irritability is vague as a diagnosis. It may come coupled with PMS, chemical imbalance, kicking addictions, or an emotional response to external influences.

The use of citrine is more directed towards symptoms as opposed to causes. It is included in the Master Blend as all imbalance is irritating!

Clay

Clay is for detoxification of the immune system.
Master Blend / General Cleanser

When we speak of using clay as an instrument of Rock-Medicine, it is always in reference to a piece of pottery that is in excess of 200 years old, because of the porous texture of clay in its natural state. At this time, all the surface and subsurface clay on Earth has been affected or contaminated by air, soil, and waterborne pollutants. Since the density factor of clay is so slight, it has absorbed all of the toxic elements over the course of time, especially the last two centuries. If, however, you use a piece of clay pottery that is over 200 years old, you are ensured against getting an impure vibration. The ancient method of making pottery was to take clay and mix it with water. The water in that time was not infiltrated by toxic human-produced waste. After a vessel or plate was fashioned, it was then sun-dried or fire-baked, and it became hard, strengthening its density factor.

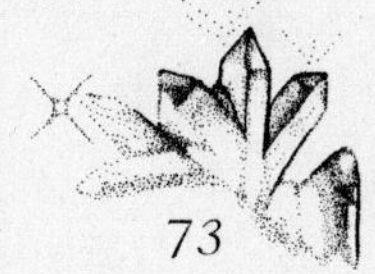

It was then no longer susceptible to the residual pollutants that have since been introduced. Luckily, man's penchant for preserving the past has afforded us vast collections of these pieces of pottery in museums and privately-held displays. Broken pieces of old pottery called potsherds can also be found in rock shops.

It is very interesting that the same clay that is now applicable in the cure of the dreaded HIV virus is also the tool that can be used to treat the common cold. Old clay is used for any condition where the immune system is adversely affected or out of balance. It is recommended that your clay be included in all general and preventive-measure applications of Rock-Medicine, due to the natural defense provided by a healthy immune system. Old clay is in the Master Blend, because our immune system is our body's first line of defense.

It seems quite appropriate that this element of healing is available to the modern world in a usable pure state only due to the development of utilitarian implements by our ancestors. In this, our past now contributes to the preservation of our future.

Pipestone may be substituted here, but the old clay is preferred.

Coal

Coal is for self-esteem.
Master Blend

This world's vast array of bodies can take no better or worse care of us than we take of them. Volcanic "pipes" of coal bear diamonds. There is no greater contrast than the brilliant light of diamonds born of pitch black. Our collective studies regarding yin/yang principles are guiding us to the conscious applications of energy, which in turn gears us toward an equal and opposite existence from that which has been so destructive to our world. Our history is our equal and opposite future. With the coming of the new age, good self-esteem puts you at one with yourself and all others in the light of loving. Self-love can be described many ways—self-discipleship, self-discipline, self-sustenance. This is the heart of survival. Life. Self-fulfillment is perpetual once self-love is activated in each individual, along with the conscious awareness that the self abiding within is the same as all that abides without. This is the significance of the terms that refer to humankind as the "Rainbow Tribe," the "Family," being "all One" and "I Am." Think of even our collective title, "human beings." With healthy self-esteem, we are fully validated, just by "being." Everything else is a celebration of that fact. What we create then is based on a preexistent joy, with natural enthusiasm.

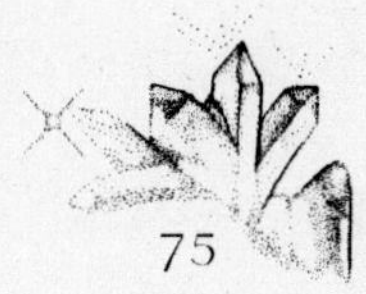

The collective self-esteem is on the rise. However, some areas are in particular emergency status, such as in teenagers, minorities, and all those who exhibit psychotic and/or antisocial behaviors. Use coal when forgiving oneself for some misdeed, for suicidal tendencies, for fear of being alone, for taking responsibility for one's own feelings, and for anyone dealing with a severe trauma as a result of a personal attack by another. This is by no means a complete list.

Clearly, coal is as multifaceted a "rock," in terms of being a healing instrument, as the diamond is in terms of sheer beauty.

Coral

Coral is for calcium-based structures, such as bone, and for calcifications.

Coral is the calcified skeleton left behind by the tiny secreting polyps from the oceans of the world. It is exactly what its appearance indicates. It is for the bone and the skeletal structure. It is also applied in instances where calcifications occur. If you combine coral with malachite, which is for the eyes, you have chemically and vibrationally described a cataract. Coral is applied in any situation involving bones.

The marrow of the bone is treated with iolite. (See **Iolite**.) The combining of calcite and coral is the obvious choice for bone cancer. If you add iolite to these two, you have indicated that the marrow is involved; add emerald, which addresses the back, and you have now described with your stone sentence the condition spinal meningitis. Coral can be applied to all bone disruptions, breaks, and calcium deposit growth on the bone itself. Weak or brittle bones will also be strengthened. This is an invaluable aid for the spectrum of bone problems suffered by the elderly (i.e., osteoporosis). The skeletal structure of anything is its base of support.

The mental aspects of correlation here are of the same nature. This is a good essence to use on small infants to add an insurance of good physical, mental, and spiritual support throughout their development. Also, coral is well applied to those diseases where the skeletal functions have either atrophied or are breaking down.

The skeleton and teeth are all the dead leave behind.

Covellite

Covellite is for radiation toxicity and
the nearly universally affected thyroid.
Master Blend / General Cleanser

Covellite is one of the most sophisticated tools in Rock-Medicine. We say this because the most advanced form of human-made toxicity is radiation. Our whole planet and its environment and atmosphere are all toxic with radiation. The planet has a natural level of radiation, which we have driven dangerously high. Industrial waste, bomb testing, and even mine activity are some of the contributing factors. As with all the other polluting agents of our world, there is no area, save the mineral kingdom, that is not at a saturation point of toxicity. Now, with the introduction of the usage of covellite to clear that imbalance, we may treat ourselves from the inside out, and from the outside in.

It is the author's recommendation that as you begin prioritizing your individualized schedule for healing, you include covellite near the top of the list. Elimination of the toxic effects of the radiation in our soil, air, water, organic matter, and animals will then leave us with a clearer view of what illnesses are left to address.

Radiation attacks the thyroid gland in a human being. This is manifested in countless symptomatic conditions. The thyroid gland is the seat of inspiration in the human body, and anxiety is produced when the thyroid is ailing. This anxiety often goes undetected and undiagnosed because of the current proportion of the masses afflicted.

One of the common residual side effects of the presence of thyroid toxicity is a condition called goiter. The patient's metabolism is involved, and a very large number of the obese who suffer from goiter are properly diagnosed with thyroid conditions. The treatment for goiter includes both the covellite for the thyroid and apatite for proper metabolism. Covellite is included in the Master Blend.

Everything, everywhere on this planet needs to be treated for radiation poisoning. We can detoxify our food as well as tainted medicinal herbs by using covellite in a focus direct. We can also use the covellite to treat other rock instruments that may be toxic due to direct exposure to radiation. Stones do not clear themselves of radiation toxicity without the application of covellite, as they will of other toxins over a three-to-four hour cleansing period. We can likewise treat our atmosphere with a power spread, bodies of water with essence, and the soil with instruments called wands. Cobaltine or cobaltite may be used instead of covellite at any time.

On January 6, 1987, the knowledge of the use of this stone came through to begin the healing of ourselves and to facilitate the purging necessary to make way and ready our heavenly inspired home.

Diamond

Diamond is for harmony and balance, consciously, in higher consciousness.
Master Blend / Shield Stone

The diamond is an important herald of the matriarchal influence of this new age. It is no coincidence, considering women's roles here and the female propensity and affinity for diamonds. They say, "Diamonds are a girl's best friend," but as it turns out, they are everybody's.

The very same moment that the first diamond came into its own perfection was the same moment in time that the first human became enlightened. Such is the precision of the correlation of our development with all that is. There are no accidents. The existence of life and its inherent growth and development is its own catalyst for being. I believe the old adage that "necessity is the mother of invention" applies fully here. We are here because we needed to be, and we survive because we need to. We will likewise be made whole with our creation, because in order for existence to continue, we need to.

Diamond is for perpetuating a constant state of what we have in the past called meditation. This is not a thing that you "do." This is a state of *being,* at all times, in 100 percent focus with all of your energies and their changing relationships to those vibrational influences with which they come into contact. The diamond application is of the state of meditation becoming a state of being. This energy puts us in touch with the awareness that we have a responsibility for our world. Too often we appease ourselves with thoughts like,

"Everything is just perfect and as it should be." This is not so. Everything is merely what it is. It will always be just what we make it.

Diamond may be safely used with any stone and for any length of time. It happens to be one of the three stones that everyone should have on their person at all times. Of the three, topaz and diamond are both suitable for constant use, while agate may be kept in one's pocket for first aid.

When combining diamond with any stone, the diamond serves to enhance and amplify that stone's ability to heal. Diamond can be a very expensive stone to acquire, but remember that the instrument you use need only be a true representation of the vibration of its family. There is no diminishment of healing virtue by way of size, color, clarity, or origin, so *any* diamond, as long as it is a true diamond, will convey the beneficial diamond influence.

Dinosaur Bone

Dinosaur bone is for waste.
Master Blend

Waste in any form is treated by this bone. This includes waste of time, waste of energy, waste of resources, wasting words, wasted efforts—the list goes on and on. You will notice this stone listed in the Master Blend.

In cases where anorexic conditions persist, the "wasting away" of the individual on all three levels is treated.

On a global scale, dinosaur bone stops the animal, vegetable, and mineral extinctions that are in progress, as well as preventing future ones.

Wasted efforts dominate our society at present. When there are conflicts, great measures of time and energy are lost.

Emerald

Emerald is for the back.

Chronic back problems are predominant in our society worldwide; however, the causes differ. Problems from injury may involve discs, muscles, and/or vertebrae. When the problem is stress-related and painful stress pockets are concentrated in the back, combine petrified wood with emerald and the Master Blend. If the problem is spinal cord injury, combine the appropriate stones as indicated.

One is sulfur, for inflammation of connective joint tissue. Another is halite, where muscle elasticity has been eroded, such as in atrophy from lack of movement during a long period of immobility, including states of coma. Halite includes the treatment of tendons and ligaments. Coral is used where the bone itself is involved or when calcium deposits are present. Iolite is used when marrow is affected.

Some neck injuries will certainly be treated with emerald, where the imbalance is directly related to or involves the connection from the base of the skull to the spinal column. This may range from actual damaged vertebrae to pinched, bruised, and severed nerves. Emerald with rhodonite says, "The nerves in the back." The spine can be likened to a zipper. When there is one area ill, the whole is effected. This is so for all of existence.

The back is a fundamental base of structural support. It indicates uprightness. It serves as a "meeting ground" for the physical body's nerves and energy flows, and so it is with the correlation of this area to emotional, mental, and spiritual support. In this age of healing, it is now widely accepted that all three of the elements, body, mind (including the emotions), and spirit, are inseparably interrelated. It stands to reason, therefore, that the presence of illness in any of the three domains denotes an equal problem manifesting in the other two. In the case of back problems, the quality of uprightness is significant in all three. It is this quality that sets humankind apart from the beasts. Walking erect and the utilization of fire are the only two abilities that gave us dominion over the planet. How will we use them now?

Fluorite

Fluorite states the presence of unwanted fluid.

Fluorite occurs in many colors. Beautiful blues, green, and various hues of purple make up the colorfully striped bands found. Specimens are sold in rough, rocklike configurations or sometimes as smooth stained-glasslike slices.

Fluorite addresses those conditions resulting in excesses of fluid. Fluorite combined with black tourmaline speaks to fluid in the lungs. This applies to pleurisy and congestion from colds or flu, as well as the more dramatic threat of infection and bronchial conditions. This stone is invaluable for prevention of either damage or chronic residuals in small children with severe congestion. Many smokers suffer from excesses of fluids in their lungs and need relief for this. The air pollution levels also predispose people to lung pollution, and where this results in lung fluid, the application of fluorite is pertinent. (See **Black Tourmaline**.)

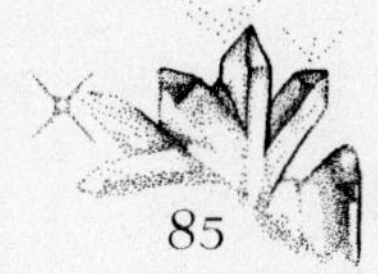

With malachite, for the eyes, and rhodochrosite, stating epidermis, you are describing a fluid-filled pustule in or around the eye, such as a sty. This application may be accomplished via essence put directly in the eye. Water on the elbow or water on the knee calls for fluorite with sulfur. This combination states, "fluid on a connective joint." With lepidolite, fluorite indicates "fluid on the brain." These are only some examples.

Fluorite Wands

Fluorite wands are impressionable for specific healing influences.

This form of fluorite constitutes a different instrument than fluorite in the rock form. The wands for common use are the little-to-large octahedral forms. Each fluorite represents an individual and complete wand. The use and application of these are the closest that we have at present to access the miracle-wielding power of ethereal control.

Fluorite wands should not be displayed for sale in an accessible way for others to touch and handle, as the means by which we activate a wand of fluorite to perform a specific healing influence is by creative desire. One merely has to take the new fluorite in hand and predispose, by thought or word, the specific need for which that instrument will be used. Thereafter, the wand is forevermore set to this vibratory level, and the same fluorite can be used by others only for the same type of malady. None of the stones are limited in any way in their ability to be used by anyone, as long as it is a correct application. In the case of fluorite wands, the person would have to need the same help as the person who set it, such as for quitting smoking or perhaps for a specific flu strain. All of the stones have a use and purpose. Some cross over in their ability to relate for healing a similar situation, and this describes the use of fluorite wands. On the other hand, there is always an optimal application for any imbalance, which is the strategic assembling of stone combinations, and this is always the desired one to use. It is much less

effective to set a fluorite for cancer than to use the calcites provided to address that illness.

Fluorite wands are best applied as personal remedies for smoking, nausea, headache, vertigo and similar phobias, motion sickness, indigestion, nail biting, and so on.

Many different "wands" are available in the metaphysical marketplace. Most if not all of them are pseudomagical interpretations of the real thing. You must use discretion, when handling or standing in the vicinity of wands, as some of these elaborately constructed art forms can in fact be dangerous. Remember always that the stones will do what they do, no matter what you believe.

As far as Rock-Medicine is concerned, the fluorite octahedrons are the only wands we are authorized to use at present!!!

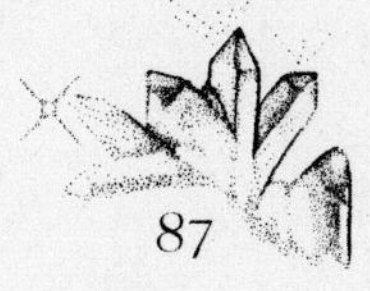

Galena

Galena is for balanced breathing.

Brilliant silver in color and boxlike in appearance, galena has a precise focus: all types of respiratory illnesses are treated with it. On the physical body, galena also works as an antihistamine. Respiratory problems include asthma, bronchitis, emphysema, and hyperventilation caused by panic or extreme physical exertion, to name a few. This stone regulates the physical rhythm of breathing to facilitate a state most conducive to that of a center of calm. This translates into the spiritual aspect of peaceful flow or serenity. The mind paces itself to the rhythm of the breath, allowing a constant resonance toward creative progress. Since we are fast transforming to acute stages of awareness on individual levels, see this mineral as a tool for the transformation of the physically earthbound self into that of your divine or Light-Being self. This process involves the ascension of our rhythm and the descent or drawing near of the divine's. This facilitates the Brahma influence.

Brahma represents one of the three divine influences that stabilize the Heaven-space to this physical plane. This is the inclusion of Heaven in the third dimension. Three points of reference make a plane exist. We emanated from Heaven, descended to Hell, and are completing the circle with ascending again to Heaven. This also points to the fact that *balance* is the guarantee and insurance of the eternal Heaven-space here.

Galena speaks to the heart of all that is debased in the state of Nevada. This is a power seat in the decline of the infrastructure of the socioeconomic system in the United States. It is the area of precedent in the taking of drugs, alcohol, and addictive behavior to their points of extreme and abusive imbalance. Nevada represents the dash for greed and the enslaving and minimizing of the virtuous value of women and minerals. The vast expanse of ground area, viewed as barren, was test-bombed instead of nurtured by us who are the garden's tenders. Nevada set precedents for the wealthy's fare, by way of others' failure. The result has been ruin through laws sanctioned by a governing organization that is self-serving to the point of reckless destruction.

The United States is still the pioneer of freedom. We are a special people because we have come together as many nations unified under the flag of devotion to freedom. We are moving quickly toward the oft-repeated scenario of revolution as long as the rhythms of fairness and equality are missing from the nation's hierarchy.

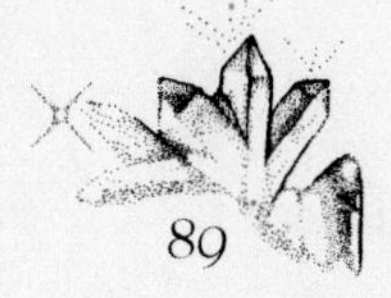

Meditation is the practice most widely-used to date by students of enlightenment. Meditation is practicing the cosmic rhythm. It affords the freedom of mind, body, and spirit, unto oneself and in interaction with all creation. This is flow. Meditation takes many forms. All the arts are meditations: music, dance, song, creative writing, swimming, fishing, hobbies and crafts, prayers, mantras, chanting, ceremonies, offerings, walks, altered states of consciousness, yoga, TM, exercise and aerobics, hypnosis, and all other trance states. Everything that we do alters our state. Even driving we get highway hypnosis!

Galena's ability to assist in the balance of rhythm is multifaceted, from its literal influence on our lungs' breathing motion to the subtle energy rhythms utilized during meditation.

Garnet

Garnet is for blood pressure.

Just as galena represents rhythm, garnet represents the strength of that rhythm.

A wide range of minerals makes up the family of garnet, ranging in color from brilliant green to deep red. The most common garnets are of the deep red variety. This stone is particularly helpful when used with hematite for the condition of hemophilia. A general application of the essence or the hand-held method will regulate and fortify the blood pressure. It is indicated for use in most situations where heart valve function is out of balance.

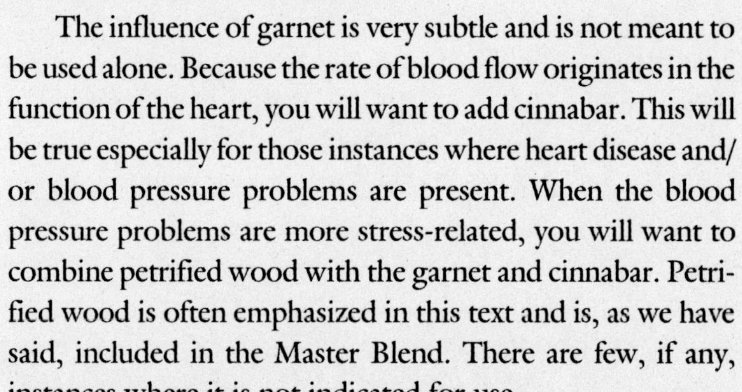

The influence of garnet is very subtle and is not meant to be used alone. Because the rate of blood flow originates in the function of the heart, you will want to add cinnabar. This will be true especially for those instances where heart disease and/or blood pressure problems are present. When the blood pressure problems are more stress-related, you will want to combine petrified wood with the garnet and cinnabar. Petrified wood is often emphasized in this text and is, as we have said, included in the Master Blend. There are few, if any, instances where it is not indicated for use.

Garnet is the stone of choice for both high and low blood pressure, as it balances the rate of force throughout the body's blood course. This is one example of how simple Rock-Medicine is. Instead of having to learn two different medications, you need only know one. This is true in many areas of use, such as green tourmaline for both high or low blood sugar.

The pressure we feel in our flow of life can be equally problematic, as our spiritual and mental rates of force are disrupted. Thus, the pace-setting device of garnet can be applied to specifically address one's discomfort of body, mind, or spirit as the universal flows accelerate.

Gold

Gold is for strength on any level.
Master Blend / Shield Stone

Gold is for strength and survival of the energy's best potential for growth and provides a particularly positive vibration. Add to gold's beauty and durability the perfection of its chemistry, and it is no wonder that the early alchemists lost their focus and regarded gold as a means of hoarding energy instead of using it as a chemical tool. Their knowledge of chemistry joined with society's pursuit of monetary wealth. It was at this juncture that the metaphysical use of minerals ceased to exist in mainstream sciences. Gold represents the influences of sustenance and growth—not excess. Gold will strengthen the positive created in the spirit and mind of an individual.

White and yellow gold make good settings for any shield stones that one chooses to use at length, as gold is appropriate for wearing. Gold will strengthen the effect not only of the stone it is touching, but will work individually for overall strength. The only safeguard you must take into consideration with gold is that piercing the skin with metals is going to have a blocking effect on the meridial flows. Any discomfort caused by the blockage may be instantly relieved by taking the jewelry off for a period of no less than ten minutes. This is a good first-aid practice for fainting, dizziness, nausea, or any medical emergency or situation. Gold is a most beneficial influence on the body for the vitals and levels of tolerance. How odd that during surgery it is one of modern medicine's standard practices to remove the patient's jewelry, usually even the gold wedding bands. However, this is in direct contradiction with Rock-Medicine's practicality. The trauma to the physical body that surgery poses makes gold one of the most beneficial influences to have present. Unfortunately, mainstream medicine tends away from such awarenesses. The separation of science and spirit is no true medicine.

Granite

Granite promotes kindness and gentleness.
Master Blend / Shield Stone

Granite represents the nature of St. Francis of Assisi, the caring for small children, and all animals. This is expanded by the use of granite to include all life-forms. We are in an ominous age of vulnerability. The delicate fabric of balance in nature has been severely damaged by cruelty and thoughtlessness. It is the equal responsibility of us all to turn the tide.

Gentleness and kindness are feminine qualities, but are often neither exemplified in the behavior of women nor absent from that of men. Granite smooths the rough and gruff tendencies that have been bred from fear and the high degree of competition by humankind for possessions and power. The solitude of struggle due to the lack of awareness of grace has resulted in a society where a kind and gentle nature has been near-suicide for those who promote it. We all need granite. Fortunately, since we are in the midst of sure redemption at this point, granite is indicated for use in all cases. As such, it is included in the Master Blend. It seems reasonable to administer blanket applications to correctional facilities (both to the inmates and the staff), as well as to most geriatric, mental health, and child care operations.

Granite is again one of those influences that is safe and a good idea to include if there is the slightest doubt as to its being needed. This earth and its inhabitants can use all the gentleness and kindness we can muster!

Halite

Halite is for the muscle.

Halite (rock salt) is particularly valuable for use by massage therapists' clients to aid in the full retention of muscle and tissue elasticity. Since it is necessary for the client to be completely relaxed in order to receive optimum benefit from this type of treatment, the best application of halite is either hand-held or via essence on a formal program, relative to the frequency of visits, prior to, not during, a session.

Even better is to have a "mini-spread" right in the room where the massage is taking place or a "focus-direct" pointed at the work table. (This setup is described in the chapter on applications.)

All forms of physical therapy, chiropractic, and sports massage are highly benefited by this influence. So, too, is any type of "patterning" or range-of-motion exercises for limbs in a state of atrophy. This stone is an excellent preventive measure for geriatric patients and victims of degenerative muscle disease. Halite is another fine influence to use on newborns or small infants to give a good foundational vibration to their growing body.

Halite is excellent for use by athletes to minimize cramps and rigidity, and it provides protection against greater degrees of injury. This applies also to those individuals who work at very strenuous physical jobs. All types of gymnasts and dancers will find halite beneficial for enhancing their performance, likewise all individuals on personal programs of fitness, including aerobics, running, jogging, or calisthenics.

Combined with rhodochrosite, it restores the tissue elasticity to those on weight loss programs. This helps eliminate "loose" skin after significant loss of weight.

As a healing influence, halite is a part of the combination of stones used to address muscular dystrophy and related syndromes. More often than not, where we find the need for sulfur (for inflammation and swelling of connective joint and muscle tissue), halite goes hand in hand.

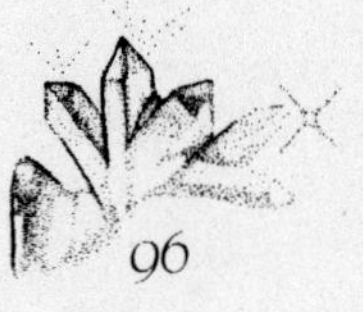

Hematite

Hematite is the blood purifier of the newest generation.
Master Blend / General Cleanser

The name is derived from the Greek word for blood, and this is exactly what it addresses. Hematite is used to treat virtually all blood infections, mutations, and disorders. From AIDS to mononucleosis, blood disorders are addressed by the essence or holding of hematite. It is included in the Master Blend as one of the seven physical cleansers. This is a new age stone, and it looks it! Hematite acts to cleanse and purify the structure of the blood in people under the age of 55 (in contrast to the use of carnelian by those over 55). The metallic cast to hematite actually looks like a newer stone, whereas the carnelian reminds us of times past with its rich orange hues.

You will notice as you study and apply this Rock-Medicine that, like the pictures in the Tarot, a rock's countenance and even name hold many clues as to its nature and consciousness.

Hemimorphite

Hemimorphite is for transformation.
Master Blend

Hemimorphite, or transformation at the base level, is applied as part of the combination for dramatic weight loss or gain, or where dramatic tumor or adhesion is present.

Transformation equates to many changes on every level. When searching for spiritual transformations, always make sure you have addressed the obvious areas of your physical and mental needs first. On the broad considerations of this stone, like many, it could be readily applied in most situations, and it is one of the stones in the Master Blend. There is no situation, when you are treating illness, wherein you do not want change. This stone acts as a spark plug for the stones' progress in healing. Remember too that change is the only constant.

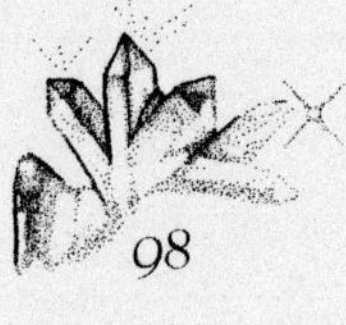

Herkimer Diamond

Herkimer diamond is for the neck. The throat, larynx, voice box, and vocal cords are all under its influence.

This stone works very well on all forms of strain, irritation, and infection of the neck area, both interior and exterior. With the proper combinations added, you can direct the "rock-sentence" to apply therapy to specific conditions. The situation may be whiplash. It may be cough and/or irritation due to cold, flu, or allergies. Damaged or atrophied vocal cords and voice box due to injury, surgery, or coma are further examples. Herkimer diamond is excellent for orators and singers, and it works with calcite on cancers in the neck and throat areas.

Consider the many possible applications on an aesthetic level, when Herkimer diamond can be used with celestite for the "voice of truth," with lava for the "voice of authority" (perfect for school teachers), or with red rock of Sedona for the "voice of the spirit," not to mention with granite for a gentle and kind vocalization.

Iolite

Iolite is for bone marrow.

This is one of the stones about which we have received the most recent information. Its use is indicated where the bone marrow is affected. This includes certain forms of cancer, where calcite, among other stones, would be added. Some blood disorders are likewise concentrated in the marrow, and the iolite works as a guide to direct healing to the bone marrow itself. Also, consider the importance of the health of the "marrow" of our spirit and mind!

Ivory

Ivory is for fertility.

The factors contributing to conditions of infertility are numerous indeed. Whether the cause is physical, mental, or spiritual is irrelevant to the use of ivory. The stones used in combination with ivory will vary per their specifics. For example, pearl, amethyst, and rhodochrosite are added in those instances where abnormal epidermal activity is a contributing factor to infertility, as is the case with plugged tubes. Also, many emotional imbalances sometimes result in infertility. These should be treated with the appropriate stone as well as with ivory.

Rock-Medicine works to heal by correcting vibrational activity in the three bodies. If a person wishes to become pregnant and is not successful in doing so, no matter what the given cause, ivory must be used in addition to other indicated treatments and procedures. Ivory's specific function is to address the lack of a state of pregnancy, regardless of its cause.

Jacinth/ Hessonite Garnet

Jacinth/Hessonite garnet is for creative visualization.

This stone can be likened to a mineral hallucinogenic, because of its influence on a visionary level. It differs from chemical or herbal applications, in that there is no residue when dealing with vibration as the catalyst. As a result, there are no "bad trips." The creative visions produced are the product of pure mental clarity.

This stone's use is another example of an advanced level of study and development and is not meant for use before having addressed one's obvious and general imbalances first.

Hand-held, in essence, or in a focus direct, jacinth will enable you to fully experience the reality of the creative mode. This was one of the stones present in Aaron's breastplate, as described in the Old Testament.

Jade

Jade is for detoxification of emotional and spiritual residuals and the resulting blockages and physical illness.
Master Blend / General Cleanser

The use of this stone goes back to ancient Egypt and China. It is known as the "side stone" or "hip stone" because of its healing properties on the kidneys. Its name, however, comes from the Spanish conquest of Central and South America, where it was traditionally used for kidney ailments. Jade means hip. (*Yu,* the Chinese word for hip, was never widely accepted as this stone's name, though it was called this early on.)

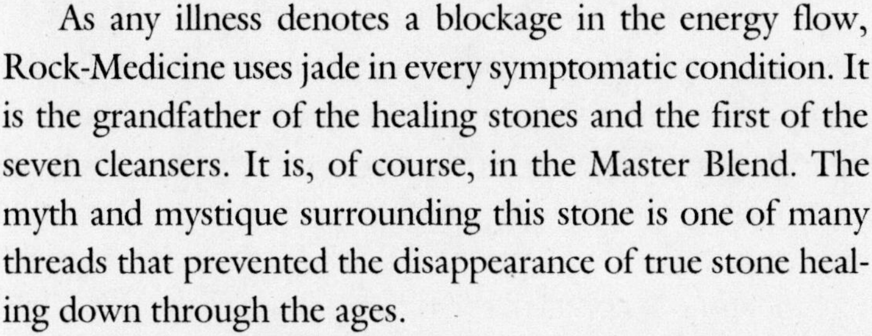

As any illness denotes a blockage in the energy flow, Rock-Medicine uses jade in every symptomatic condition. It is the grandfather of the healing stones and the first of the seven cleansers. It is, of course, in the Master Blend. The myth and mystique surrounding this stone is one of many threads that prevented the disappearance of true stone healing down through the ages.

As with agate, jasper, and other stones, the color of jade used and the quality are not factors in its use or application. Jade is jade is jade, no matter what, as long as its chemical composition is in the nephrite jade family. Rough, uncut, and unpolished jade is preferred. However, as with other stones, use what you have rather than not beginning the healing process at all. You may even use an ornately carved piece.

Jade may be applied in various ways other than the usual essence or hand-held methods. One of these has to do with tension headaches. For this purpose, the influence seems to work more efficiently when the jade is applied to either of the temples and/or the middle of the forehead, wherever the pain is felt most. Another variation of use is any time a noticeable degree of heat or fever is present in the affected area. The patient then applies the jade directly to the area for a period of twenty minutes. This kind of topical application seems to work well in many different instances for immediate relief from pain/fever. A good example of this is using jade and halite or sulfur, applied directly to the back. For relief from the pain of arthritis, use jade with sulfur, directly on the area. The jade will feel very hot from its absorption of toxicity and must then be left to clear before being used for another application, essence, or placement in a spread. This clearing process takes three hours.

Jade is also a very good stone to be used preventively.

Individuals in a wide spectrum of activities and professions can benefit by using jade as a part of their routine. Some examples are those in the mental health fields and most all high "burnout"-related work, that is, anywhere there is extensive use of chemical, emotional, or residual elements. Always, with any application of Rock-Medicine, be sure to note the stone or crystal of choice in addition to the jade. One such instance might be an X-ray technician, who would want to use covellite for the presence of radiation and jade to negate toxic levels of radiation saturation. There are no applicable safeguards, except to take care to use a cleared stone and to remove it within the given twenty-minute time frame.

Remember, jade is useful in all physical applications of Rock-Medicine.

Jasper

Jasper is a shield stone for positive outcomes.
Master Blend / Shield Stone

Confrontation does not always mean conflict. Any time you enter into an encounter with others, you are confronting their energy. Jasper works to cause all outcomes to be in one's best interest. This may not always be the thing one desires as the result, but rather what the cosmos sees as the best situation for you.

Jasper is applicable when going into job interviews, business presentations, and legal solicitations. When using the influence of jasper for legal confrontations, it is advisable to include amazonite, which is for good judgment.

The list of uses of Jasper is virtually limitless. Jasper is one of the shield stones, which may be safely worn or used at all times, as its function is to influence and not as a detoxifier. Regardless of your feelings about the elicited results, the presence of jasper ensures that it is for the best. One of the first lessons we learn as children is that what we want is not always what we need. Be assured that the use of jasper not only ensures the outcome to be in your best interest but also in the best interest of all concerned. This never gives one person an advantage over another, because we are all connected, and what is best for one in any given situation is best for all involved. This is the closest stone we have to what might be considered a luck stone.

Kunzite

Kunzite is for surrender.
Master Blend

When we speak of surrender, it applies to a vast spectrum of situations. One good example would be finding oneself in a living or working space that is unrewarding or unfulfilling, yet in which one must remain while pursuing or preparing for alternatives. In the course of losing a battle, such as a debate or argument, even to the point of having to call upon oneself to deliver an apology, kunzite is most helpful. Be mindful of the subtle differences in the two concepts of loss and surrender, for the two are very close in nature. Refer to the material provided on rose quartz for further help in determining appropriate applications. Kunzite is like the serenity prayer in mineral form.

Lapis Lazuli

Lapis is to strengthen the attitude or spirit that is about you, and for use in the spreads as a transmitter.
Master Blend / Women's Hormonal Balance

This beautiful blue rock is one of our most powerful influences and should always be used with the greatest of care. Often confused with sodalite, there is one sure way of determining its true family, and that is by the presence of pyrite in the surface of the stone. This presence is most important, though, for emphasizing, in an undeniable fashion, the importance of setting lapis in no metal other than gold. It is so dangerous to put this stone in any other metal that lapis itself carries a constant reminder and indicator in its very appearance. It has always seemed incredible to this author that, with the obvious presence of the gold-toned pyrite, any intelligent person could put lapis in silver. As you refer to the safeguards recommended regarding silver, you can see clearly the negative ramifications of this.

As stated, lapis will strengthen the attitude or spirit that is about you. This needs to be regarded very carefully, since one can have a spirit of anger, a spirit of sickness, a spirit of addiction, a spirit of depression, etc. Therefore, evaluate one's spirit carefully before opting to intensify its vibration through the use of this mineral.

The Ten Commandments were written on lapis. This is the stone that serves as a footrest at the throne of God, as described in the story of Moses' encounter on the mountain. The philosophers' stone is also of lapis. Many objects of spiritual antiquity were of this stone, although their descriptions have been mistranslated and called sapphire.

Historically, many translucent to opaque blue rocks were all called sapphires, and they ranged from true sapphire to lapis lazuli.

For female hormone imbalance, a triad of stones applies, just as with the combination of three for male hormone imbalance. When used in combination with opal and pearl, lapis balances the female hormones. Used in this combination, the lapis becomes altered to the specific application of the triad and poses no danger of strengthening a contraindicated attitude or spirit. These male/female combinations work as a team of three in each case, as well as each stone having individual uses. The lapis is for matriarchal aspects that are inherent to the female physical, emotional, and spiritual system. This combination, as we've said, is a logical starting point for the use of Rock-Medicine in a woman's cleansing process.

When using lapis as a transmitter of long distance healing, the spread must be ringed with lapis. The strand used should be strung on nonmetallic cord and is inhibited by the presence of a metal clasp. Such a strand is, fortunately, not difficult to find, as many bead workers choose this continuous method of stringing many stones and gems. (See the section on spreads for additional specifics.)

Very important safeguards must be kept in mind regarding the use of this stone. First of all is the obvious one, of recognizing those times when the spirit is one that is not deserving of amplification. As with clear quartz, you will want to take it off if you are wearing it alone and an ill spirit arises. Also, using lapis on someone who has latent emotional or psychological problems that can surface spontaneously may be dangerous, for the patient may not be ready or equipped to handle the resultant onset of those problems. Lapis has a high saturation level. It can quite literally burn someone if used to excess. We've seen instances of rash or skin eruption that bear this out. If you find yourself having over-applied lapis, the antidote is the stone sugelite or louvelite, as it is also called. Any of the first three methods of application may be used, in any combination, for your four times a day. Remember, only the shield stones can be used for more than twenty minutes at a time. However, when lapis is worn with other stones, it serves to strengthen the spirit of those stones instead of yours, because it resonates to its own kind first. Gold and lapis are quite complementary to each other and can be worn in combination as a shield.

Lava

Lava is for command of authority.

This is one stone whose true use has been carefully guarded throughout the ages. It is for the safeguarding of the strong vibration of lava that all of the mysticism and superstition concerning the removal of pieces from the islands of Hawaii has been propagated. Even in these modern times, you can go to various museums and lava parks in Hawaii and find letters from literally every type of personality, from the most conservative to the most liberal. Their letters are of apology and to return the pieces that they took. Many people are convinced that the lava brought them bad luck because they took it without permission or invitation by the goddess Pele.

This is a remarkable occurrence, when you consider the aspects concerning volcanoes themselves. I'm sure you would tend to agree with me that few things can command the attention of humankind like an erupting volcano. So, too, is the influence of lava. The key to its use is being granted some position of authority in the first place. The range is quite vast. One may have authority over a classroom, an office, a project or committee, or even a country and its armies. Now, lava could contribute to a volatile situation, for it does not distinguish between good and bad intentions on the part of the one who is seeking to better implement his authority or position of authority. Just imagine if someone like Hitler had the benefit of lava's power working on his behalf. Even greater disaster than what ensued could have been the result. This information is still to be used and guarded judiciously.

On the average level of application, one may use lava to be a better leader, guide, teacher, boss, and parent. When combined with other stones, such as Herkimer diamond, you can exact a voice of authority, or add red rock of Sedona, as the author of this text did during writing, to produce the voice of spiritual authority.

Do not hesitate to use this wonderful stone, but exercise a reasonable amount of care in its application, and keep your motives good.

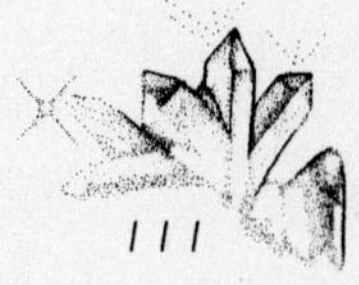

Lepidolite

Lepidolite is for the brain.

Often found as the matrix for pink tourmalines, this lavender stone is a lithium-based crystal and water-soluble. Therefore, it may not be used in an essence. The applications of this stone include the hand-holding of a set crystal, spreads, or focus direct.

The most obvious use of this stone is for manic-depression where there is a lithium imbalance. Any and all instances of brain-chemical disorder are treated with lepidolite. Head injury and brain contusion are two very important occasions to include this element's influence, and likewise conditions of chemical dependency, which call for the administration of lepidolite to balance the brain's chemical confusion. When brain infection, lesions, or adhesions occur in AIDS patients, lepidolite is included with the combination of stones for AIDS. The heavy prescribing of various psychotropic drugs by current medical practitioners has caused a high degree of residual toxicity, which is counteracted by lepidolite. Comatose patients need lepidolite during the coma state, as a preventative measure for minimizing brain dysfunction. Pregnant women who are using prescribed drugs can use lepidolite to ensure the brain-chemical balance in the unborn fetus, as well as to treat the infant, post-delivery. Since lepidolite says "brain," it will be in your stone combinations any time the brain is involved. Another example is to combine it with fluorite for water or fluid on the brain. If cancerous tumors are on the brain, lepidolite serves to direct the rest of the minerals to that area. The balance of the brain's

chemicals is essential to our proper functioning as we enter the age of more consciously using our mental powers. Thinking is our primary function. It is important to remember that you are treating the body's brain as well as the mind's brain and spirit's brain. Think about that!

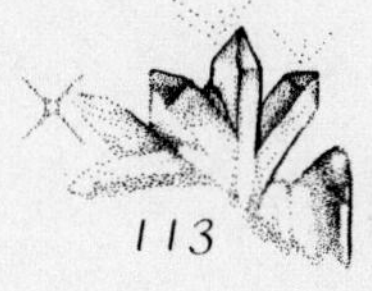

Magnetite

Magnetite is for reversing the polarity of a situation.

This is a dramatic and extreme vibration. It causes the electric polarization of a situation to effect a 180-degree turnabout. Understandably, the applications are relatively few. This stone is the mineral equivalent to euthanasia. Magnetite produces quite literally a "cure it or kill it" result. It is suggested that you do not opt to use this application based on information, but rather on a test of kinesiology to determine whether or not it is appropriate to use. Muscle-testing overrides the conscious mind's presuppositions and delivers diagnostic information from the subconscious level.

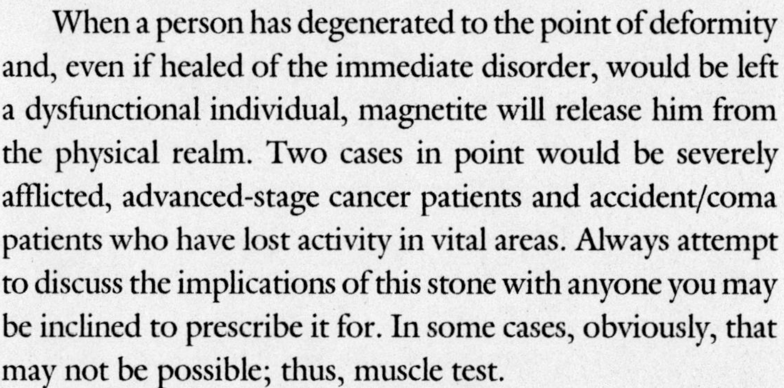

When a person has degenerated to the point of deformity and, even if healed of the immediate disorder, would be left a dysfunctional individual, magnetite will release him from the physical realm. Two cases in point would be severely afflicted, advanced-stage cancer patients and accident/coma patients who have lost activity in vital areas. Always attempt to discuss the implications of this stone with anyone you may be inclined to prescribe it for. In some cases, obviously, that may not be possible; thus, muscle test.

The flip side to the use of magnetite is that, used in the course of grave illness, it causes an immediate reversal of the injurious polarity. Magnetite is one of the fastest acting Rock-Medicine instruments! It has the potential to snatch one back from the grasp of death or to catapult one into it. The first of the three times that I have used magnetite in the last fourteen years was in a Sparks, Nevada emergency room. The young woman lay there with football-sized tumors erupting from her shoulders, neck, and underarms. The dimly lit room could not hide the neon yellow of her jaundiced skin. Her doctors had given her a prognosis of another nine months of life. There was no question in my mind that I would trust only the result of muscle-testing to determine the application. Out of forty stones, she tested to need only two—jade for the release of blocks and magnetite for the complete polarity reversal of the vibration. Her limbs were so twisted that the only place she could hold the stone was under her armpit. So she did. She died two days later.

One of the most elusive imbalances in existence is the suicidal tendency. We as a planet have embarked on a mission of destruction. We have veiled it behind the facade of patriotism and capitalism. This disguise has kept the self-destructive behavior at a subconscious level. To consider, on a conscious level, the taking of one's own life requires the utmost in both courage and daring, as well as the total failure of one's survival instinct. This is a true paradox.

We have two types of suicidal personalities. One is the individual who merely desires attention and usually ensures that he is rescued. If he dies, it is, more often than not, an accident. This group is not who magnetite is for. The second type is a tricky condition to recognize. This is the one who commits suicide to the astonishment of those closest to him, the soul who executes himself without giving any clear-cut cry for help. It is part of this thought process's nature to make the victim virtually unrecognizable. The opportunity to apply magnetite to these in need is usually after the fact, and then only in the case of failure or interruption of a serious attempt, which gives us the proverbial second chance. When in doubt, with suicide, use it, because it is better to have it and not need it than to need it and not have it.

Remember, these stones are doing their job to balance things. They are programmed to seek their resonant vibration and guide it to the highest level of well-being.

Malachite

Malachite is for the eyes.

This soft, green, banded, easily-carved stone is often found in copper mines and is a copper ore. Proper vision on the mental and spiritual levels is what enables us to perceive a better world. You have only to see it to have it! You create your existence. Malachite is a predecessor to enacting creative desires and making positive changes on a planet-wide scale. It is important to understand that the three bodies of existence—physical, mental, and spiritual—are inseparable. So, too, are the imbalances manifested in them. If you do not see correctly on the physical level, know that in correlation to that physical sight problem, the mental and spiritual visualization is off. Though rock medicine has its limitations and may not restore sight to one who is blind or hearing to one who is deaf, it will balance the mind and spirit in the coinciding areas.

"Faithful" application means not missing any applications! Since Rock-Medicine works like antibiotics, on a saturation-level of vibration, it is imperative that all uses of these methods be performed as prescribed, without fail. It can take as little as three weeks or up to several months to correct astigmatisms, cataracts, and other imbalances, depending on their longevity, severity, and the age of the patient.

Malachite is the stone in the sentence that denotes that the area affected is the eyes. You will add other appropriate stones based on the other elements involved. Cataracts, for instance, are treated with a combination of the Master Blend, amethyst for cell division, and coral to work with the presence of calcium deposits. For those situations where muscle weakness is the cause of poor vision, halite is essential to the combination, as is the Master Blend. Rhodonite may be indicated if nerve damage or weakness is also present. Irritation and pustules in the eye, such as a sty, call for malachite, Master Blend, fluorite, and amethyst.

Not "seeing" properly is a contributing factor to many dangerous misconceptions and delusions. No one person's clarity of vision is more important than the next; however, we can see where those in a higher position of authority pose a greater threat to the health and welfare of the whole when they are without truth in their vision.

Moldavite

Moldavite is for all fungus-related imbalances.

Much controversy surrounds this relatively new mineral element, which is not surprising, since the area of resonance with which it relates is so elusive. While fungus extracts, penicillin for one, are being used successfully to treat many common maladies, they can pose a threat as well. Moldavite in combination with barite is the stone of choice for such conditions as candida, skin fungi, tinea, and yeast infections. All of these have additional symptoms, such as irritation, which calls for the influence of citrine, or rhodochrosite, indicating skin. Clay and smoky quartz are for the purification of body fluids, while rhodochrosite and amethyst are for skin or surface-related fungi.

When evaluating the condition of fungal invasion, it is important to use the full spectrum of stones required. Athlete's foot and ringworm are two more areas of application.

Moldavite is being heralded as providing everything from enlightenment to the ability to fly. We just cannot seem to accept simply being here on earth. Since this stone arrived in a meteor, we discount its practical use and spin tales of exaggeration. Fungus is alien to this heaven place. We created it and therefore needed a tool from another space to combat it. Don't make the all too common mistake of throwing the message out in deference to elevating the messenger. This would truly be history repeating itself. Look at the way humankind has revered and even worshipped such teachers as Jesus, Mohammad, and Buddha, while never truly applying themselves to following these prophets' examples.

Moonstone (Labradorite)

Moonstone (Labradorite) is for PMS-related syndromes and for regular monthly emotional upset.
Master Blend

This white or pinkish chatoyant stone is one of the minerals commonly found in granite. It is also called spectrolite.

Men as well as women have dramatic responses to the moon's changing phases, as it affects the individual metabolism. It is generally more evident in the emotions and behaviors of women. We call this Pre-Menstrual Syndrome (PMS). Along with the triad of stones for female hormone balance, moonstone is added to eradicate the disrupting effects of premenstrual stress.

Labradorite is essentially for combating the effects of the moon's phases. As we are primarily made up of water, when the moon goes through its phases, our bodies experience tides. Men may choose to use moonstone when they notice particular difficulty at certain times during their own monthly cycle of activity. In men it is not necessarily the same sequence of days that these effects are evident. Women have the occurrence of menses as another indicator of these changes. Moonstone can be included in a daily-application essence, as a preventative measure by both sexes. You may want to include petrified wood for emotional balance in extreme cases.

As the moon shines only by the reflected light of our sun, it represents the analogy of women's reflective capacity for men's energies and, likewise, the matriarchal reflecting the patriarchal qualities. As we move into the matriarchal age, the cycles of changes will increase their intensity, and protection by the moonstone will ease the tendency to overload.

Labradorite is the true moonstone. Other common moonstones with pink, pale gray to white coloring are actually ungraduated star sapphires and are not to be confused with true moonstone.

Mother-of-Pearl

Mother-of-pearl is for strengthening of the womb.

Mother-of-pearl is used for difficult or threatened pregnancies in those women who have a history of miscarriage or stillbirths. It is suggested for use by those who are facilitating pregnancy by alternative medical methods, such as *in vitro* fertilization. Late-in-lifers are always recommended to use mother-of-pearl, as it protects them—also because the health of the fetus is a direct reflection of the health of the mother and vice versa. It is wonderful that it can work both ways.

In the event that a woman has required stitching to reinforce the cervix, it is crucial that mother-of-pearl be applied to strengthen the area.

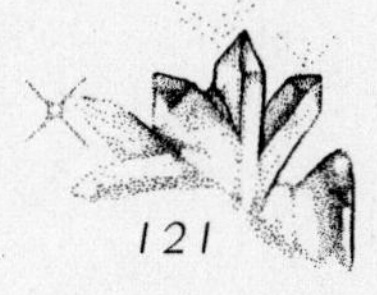

This instrument is one of emergency measures when threat of a miscarriage is present. This is especially good for ill-positioned uteruses and for cervical muscle weakness.

Likewise, sometimes we are "pregnant" with an inspiration or a thought. This would bring the mental and spiritual aspects of mother-of-pearl into play.

Obsidian

Obsidian is for prophecy.

This stone is volcanic glass and not a true crystal at all. Frequently black or grayish, certain varieties have a silver or golden sheen, just under the surface, called adjulescence.

Prophecy, of course, is not a malady but rather a sometimes-desired condition by those seeking to tune in to being of more assistance to the cosmic service corps. In the past, the choice to be one of those using the gift of prophecy has come due to the being's prior contract with the Creator before taking the earth-plane form. Prophecy is a gift as opposed to an ability. The difference between the two can be seen in the analogy of singing. We all have the ability to sing, but we do not all necessarily sound good doing so. That requires the gift. The gift of prophecy sometimes surfaces spontaneously and without conscious preparation on the part of the individual. We are in times of great change as we mesh the cosmic consciousness with our own conscious capacity.

Obsidian does not create the gift of prophecy. If the gift of prophecy is present, obsidian hones and tunes it. If one desires the prophetic ability, the use of obsidian causes him to enter into a state of receptivity to it. Obviously, this type of work comes only after one has dealt with the presence of imbalances and maladies evident in one's existing state. Such is also the case with red beryl for psychic development and jacinth for creative visualization. We must learn to be well at a walk before we run.

Prophesy is the ability to act as the audible voice of things to come. This ability to look into the future serves many uses.

We can better prepare for impending natural disasters, warn others regarding the dangerous effects of certain actions, and learn from negative attitudes without having to manifest them into reality. Most important, though, prophesy enables us to rest assured as to our guaranteed future, heaven on earth, so that it will serve to encourage others to facilitate its expeditious return.

The Creator's promise of salvation for his children is intact, and it is up to all of us whether we will have it sooner or later. Whether it is black, snowflake, mahogany, rainbow, needles, or Apache tears, all obsidian serves us as we advance through physical wellness and beyond.

Onyx

Onyx shields from intense energy exchange.
Master Blend / Shield Stone

Onyx is a two-way shield. Those who have intense energy at times may be unaware of the overwhelming effect that they have on the sensitivities of others. They would do well to protect their fragile brothers and sisters by wearing onyx to keep that energy contained. Likewise, the empaths and those among us with "open" chakras need onyx to protect against being inundated by the needy sponging of others. Onyx does not remove the ability to have these energy exchanges, it merely puts them under your conscious control. It prevents the exchange from occurring without your knowledge and forethought.

Though you may view the list of available Rock-Medicine influences as entirely valuable, by no means are all the stones indicated for use at all times.

Opal

Opal is for the elimination of fear or the denial of one's divine calling.
Master Blend / Shield Stone / Women's Hormonal Balance

All of the superstition surrounding opals throughout the ages is for good reason. They are indicative of the heavy influence the stone has with regard to the area of self-actualization. The elimination of fear and hesitancy to be at our optimal level of existence is in the domain of the opal.

Just as we have experienced delegation of authority and its abuses on the earth plane, so now are we obtaining control and the usage of our individual cosmic authorities. Whenever there is motion of any kind in the universe, whether it be light, thought, or body, that force is the force of creation. It becomes the leading edge, so to speak. This position is the guidance system. Opal represents the conscious decision to let go to the God-consciousness in each one.

Seeing one's pure potential has awed, fatefully at times, some of the greatest creative leadership to date. Many have burrowed away and hidden from the miracle they saw in themselves and the daring to dream such dreams of heavenly conscious existence. However, the current generations will bring this miracle in. The influence of opal is the remedy for all peoples who are seeking to offer themselves in service to the spirit of well-being, and were afraid to ask.

Pearl

Pearl is for the female reproductive system and for nurturing.
Women's Hormonal Balance

This beautiful luminous gem is one of the few formed in another living creature. Pearl is also the third in the triad of stones for female hormone balance. The other two are opal and lapis.

The utilization of pearl is as a general directive toward the reproductive system. If, for example, ovarian cysts are present, you would use the pearl to direct the influences of amethyst and rhodochrosite to the area for proper tissue cell mitosis. This is what is meant by using pearl as a directive. Likewise, it is used with white calcite to address cancer in the reproductive area.

Pearl is a fortifier of the female reproductive organs. However, this is not the stone of choice for infertility, which is ivory. Procreation is the means by which we have populated this planet. For some, it is an effortless venture. For others, it is a tenuous balance of fragile imperfections of physical and emotional design. Men do not use either pearl or mother-of-pearl, though it will not harm them. It is similar to the equation of peridot being only felt or effective when interacting with an enlightened individual. So it is that only women have a correlating band of vibratory rate equal to that present in pearl.

Such was woman's set assignment. Men and the patriarchal system are what gave the matriarchal guidelines their credence when, in the proverbial garden, they put the responsibility on the woman and did not take responsibility for their own actions. This set the dangerous tone for what became the imbalanced patriarchal power seat.

Pearl and mother-of-pearl are stones used exclusively by women, and both are the product of a living creature. This is a fitting correlation to the action that sets womankind apart from mankind, that of childbearing.

In our Biblical creation stories, man gave all things his name, and woman came out of the side of the man. This analogy is closely adhered to in nature. Look at the brilliant plumage of a male bird, yet these are only the trappings that lead to procreation. The nature of our culture is to defer to male identification, even to the point of taking their names. This is now changing as the matriarchal influences come to the forefront. The third-dimensional existence is based upon the dovetailed existence of the mind, body, and spirit. We must also see the triad of father, mother, and child in balance within each of us.

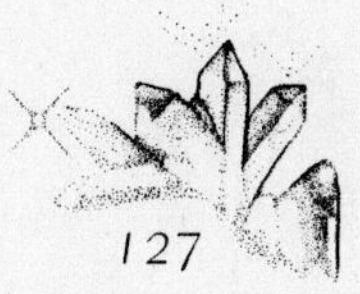

The pearl is the capstone of Rock-Medicine. In its vibration we see the birth of Light energy in a physical form that produces a rainbow luster. Its essence is instinctive maternal nurturing wisdom, above price, eventually breeding the freedom that emerges from such loving care. The matriarchal system, brought in by the conscious presence of the holy spirit of Love, is well-represented in the "hen mothering" of constant care for one's young, being happy and satisfied and with a smile of satisfaction. When this constant care is excessive or overprotective, true freedom is stifled, and pearl can also help balance this tendency. Men and women were mutually involved in this process of creating a patriarchal system, out of which its counterpart of "bride" could emerge from its "side." The matriarchal system was the birth from that exchange. This feminine principle in its ideal is about all things being at one with their own individuality, and the wisdom to see that only through nurturing with Love the physical, mental, and ethereal higher values can we prepare ourselves for THE GREAT EVENT by way of this GREAT WORK.

The pearl protects and sustains us all in the cosmic womb.

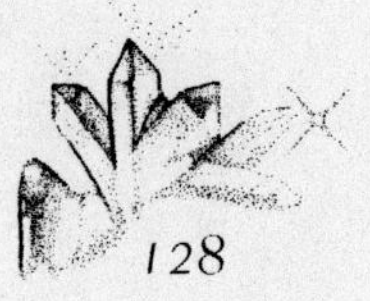

Peridot

Peridot is for the comfort of the enlightened.

Peridot, or olivine, is a green gemstone that is readily available. It is inexpensive and is not, by any means, rare. The famous green sand beach in Hawaii is comprised of crystals of peridot rolled smooth by the ocean waves. Peridot can be found as beads, inexpensive polished stones, and faceted gems.

This tool came into its most important use at the dawn of the New Age. Just prior to the Harmonic Convergence, the vibration of peridot came forth to comfort those who were first to experience the "quickening." The quickening is the term we use for the acceleration of enlightenment. As individuals "wake up," they are bombarded with feelings of exhilaration as well as fear. Peridot is like a security blanket to a small child. It assists in calming the conscious mind to the revelations of the subconscious. All knowing of good and ill resides in the subconscious, that vast percentage of our brain that we do not use. Enlightenment, or revelation, is the utilization of the portion of our mental capacity that incorporates kindness. As I've said before, there are no levels of enlightenment. Either the light is off or it is on.

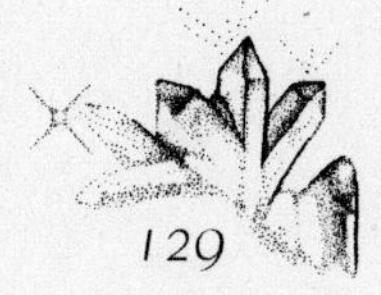

Once the light is on—once you acquire the consciousness of the light of kindness—you are faced with a whole new regimen in life. This can pose discomfort. There is the sense of overwhelm when you observe the cruelty of all who are not awake, and how many of them there are. Then there is the sense of self-loathing while considering your own deeds. Add to this the heightened sensation such as telepathy and prophetic vision. Some experience a pressure or a sense of urgency at the crown of their head. This is a valid physiological effect. We are bringing everlasting Heaven into the third or physical plane. This state is locked in our subconscious where time does not exist as we know it. You cannot create something you cannot see, just as you cannot go somewhere that you cannot find. Therefore, we must remember the heaven state.

Since Creator is the ultimate scientist, we may well expect Heaven to ride in on the winds of technology. Rock-Medicine is one of the transition technologies. Only with the merging of science and spirit in our technological advances will we continue the work to achieve Heaven on Earth!

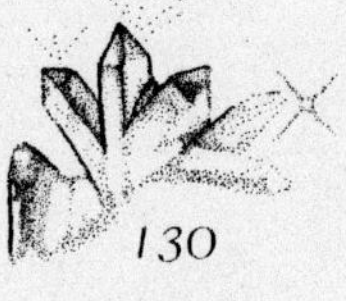

Peridot is for the comfort of the enlightened, as they go through these changes. It is not used by those who are sleeping. This is like selenite being used for childhood fears for the human individual, only peridot is for the child that is our collective consciousness. Peridot eases the pressure.

Petrified Wood

Petrified wood is for stress.
Master Blend / Shield Stone

This ancient fossil of wood is one of the best tools for emergency measures as well as for constant protection. Use it for immediate relief of emotional upheaval, anxiety attacks, despair, feelings of helplessness, anger, and so on. Petrified wood is a shield stone and so can be worn continuously. Any emergency worsens with stress trauma. Petrified wood, the agatized stem tissue of trees, will balance emotional extremes and avert numerous stress-related cardiac situations.

The applications of this stone include, of course, the optimal hand-held method. Petrified wood is a good addition to all essences and is essential in blanket spreads. It is one of the Master Blend stones.

To break up a fight situation or handle a trauma incident across a room, one may use a focus direct. One must have a clear field of aim directly at the parties involved, with no one and nothing obstructing that directional path. Holding the petrified wood against the quartz for focus and amplification, direct the stream of vibrational influence, which will be coming right out of the point (tip or tips) of the quartz, at your target. This practice is one of the most intensely dramatic displays of Rock-Medicine's capacities. So many illnesses and imbalances are the direct result of concentrated stress levels. This author suggests that everyone wear a piece of petrified wood around their neck and wear it always against the skin. In these times, reducing stress is the best beginning step on the path toward heaven and healing.

Pyrite

Pyrite is for air purification.
Master Blend / General Cleanser

Fool's gold, as pyrite is commonly called, has a boxlike configuration to its crystal structure. It is very similar to galena in appearance, except for its gold color, whereas galena has a silver cast. Pyrite is also a means of identifying lapis. Small flecks or veins of pyrite appear throughout most pieces of good quality lapis.

Pyrite is very beneficial to use in a spread where airborne pollutants are present. This can be either in a private residence where a smoker lives, or in a factory that has a form of production that lends itself to a toxic presence in the air. This also includes global air pollution.

Pyrite purifies the oxygen in our bodies and in our environment. It doesn't just clean the air in our orifices but purifies all the oxygen in our cells. It works on animals and all members of the vegetable kingdom as well. It is included for this reason in the Master Blend.

In addressing air pollution, the most effective method to use is a blanket spread. The distance you are covering is related, of course, to the power of the amplification system (see blanket spread). This is a very important treatment worldwide, and we all need all the assistance we can get.

The human-made pollutants were not here the last time the Divine presence visited this space. We must ready the air quality for Its sake, as much as our own, since we are inseparable in the state of oneness. We have all the proof we need to concede that pollution of air and water is most detrimental to the health and well-being of the mind, body, and spirit of the whole planet. Because of the severity of the pollution levels, our animal and vegetable kingdoms are in an extremely vulnerable position. Many necessary herbs and flower remedies are still needed as instruments, and yet they are toxic themselves because of the total pollution of our environment. Efforts should be made to facilitate the use of hydroponics, with sterile air and water, in order to provide the proper quality of these vegetable kingdom influences. Pyrite was one of the first tools for which we were given information regarding its use, for obvious reasons.

Quartz Crystal – Clear

Clear quartz crystal amplifies.

When we say clear quartz, we are referring to the absence of color and not the ultimate clarity of the quartz itself.

Quartz crystals amplify anything with which they come into contact, including thoughts, imbalances, wellness, other stones, etc. These simple mineral growths caught the children's eyes and started us looking at the value of beauty and enlightenment. Since they do amplify, a steady stream of misconceptions exists concerning their abilities.

Using a clear quartz with any administration of vibrational work will amplify the effort. Likewise, the influence of quartz on ailing conditions will amplify the illness and its effects.

Clear quartz has great value in Rock-Medicine as it can be set to be a surrogate of any other instrument. To obtain these surrogate instruments, the quartz is placed so that it touches the source vibration. This source vibration can be a single stone, a combination of stones, or some essence water. The important points here are that the crystal touches the source for a minimum of three hours. Once the clear quartz is physically removed from the source, it is the same as that source energy, equally as strong. It "becomes" a piece of the stone or stones it was touching. It will hold its charge only for three hours unless it is put in water. If not, it will clear itself again in three hours time. The essence thus can be used both to continuously charge the set crystal or to make additional ones. The crystal may be removed from the water after three hours, and the vibration remains in the water indefinitely. For setting additional crystals, simply add more clear crystals to the water. I often mail people crystals in bottles of water. If you are hand-holding the set stone, it may be put back with the combination you have set it to after use. Here it will cleanse and recharge for three hours. Please note that these set crystals can not be used as the stone portion of a focus direct. Likewise, except for part of the lapis ring, they may not be used as the stone portion of a blanket spread.

This "setting" is a wonderful remedy for the rarity of some minerals, their cost, and the need for obtaining quantities of Rock-Medicine tools.

The degree of amplification afforded by any given crystal or cluster is directly proportional to its size. The larger the clear crystal, the larger its parameters of influence. When using your clear quartz in long distance spreads, the more clear quartz you add, the greater the range of application. When using a focus direct, the stones must be touching the crystal at the same time it is being directed at the person or persons being treated. Whenever you pass through the point-path of a clear crystal, that is touching other stones, you get "zapped" with a laser-like stream of energy. When a ring of lapis is added, that transmitter's influence changes the clear crystal to a blanket application over the distance proportionate to the amount of amplification available.

A future function of clear quartz crystal is seen already in our strong penchant for wearing them as pendants about our necks. When clear quartz crystal is worn in a mineral-conscious community, it is a testimonial by the wearer that all is well with him that day. Should you not be well, this fact can be recognized immediately by all of us who surround you and are directly affected by your wellness. We will have domestic healthcare that is oriented toward preventive medicine, and the absence of your crystal would signify that help is needed. If, however, you should travel out in an imbalanced state while wearing your crystal, because of the very nature of the clear quartz, its function of amplification will quickly and ultimately bring to the surface the deception. Whenever you feel less than happy, healthy, and loving, you should always take off your clear quartz crystals. When you are wearing other minerals on your person, the clear quartz crystal amplifies itself first, the other minerals second, and only in the absence of another mineral's touch will it amplify whatever the given situation may be. Quartz crystal is a powerful tool, but it is rarely, if ever, going to be used alone.

Quartz Crystal – Rose

Rose quartz brings comfort and joy
at times of sorrow over loss.
Master Blend / Shield Stone

Rose quartz has been one of the first of the instruments of Rock-Medicine to be collected by the masses. This pale pink beauty has the nature of comfort in its vibration. It works particularly well for those suffering grief over the death of a loved one. It will actually stop the hurt and tears.

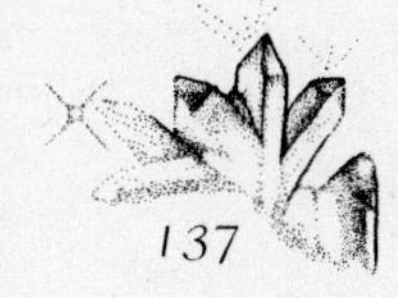

Grief over loss covers a much broader spectrum of events than one might imagine. Loss can be the loss of a job, home, or the loss of a goal, a project, or an item of importance or value. Also included are the loss of a pet or children leaving home under the many circumstances by which this might occur. These are just some of the more obvious of the infinite examples of loss.

An example that may not be so evident would be the loss of something that one has been reluctant to let go of, for whatever reason. Some examples of this include the loss of a bad habit or addiction that you have been consciously or subconsciously holding onto. Even the loss of weight calls for the use of rose quartz. Two very common instances that merit the application of this stone are the loss of anger and/ or any negative attitude. Anger is the way that the heart and mind defend themselves against hurt feelings turning to illness or despair. When situations occur in one's life that cause disruption and incline one toward hopelessness, this defense mechanism kicks in to safeguard the loss of self-worth and manifests itself as anger. Our survival instinct causes us to become angry as opposed to feeling defeated. This is particularly true of interpersonal conflicts accompanying a romantic relationship.

Fortunately, because the adage "the truth hurts" is so often the case, we have this instrument of rose quartz to ease us through the difficult yet inevitable changes that occur in our daily lives. When we are corrected or criticized appropriately and our ego will not step aside for the input to be processed in a positive and progressive manner, rose quartz will open up the appropriate receptors to facilitate the assimilation of grateful acceptance.

The best method for the use of rose quartz is the hand-held method, since the use of this stone is so often an "on call" or "as needed" type of application. That is not to say the essence cannot be used or is not effective, it's just that the use of the stone, itself, is the most expeditious manner to elicit immediate relief. It is a shield stone and is also included in the Master Blend.

Quartz Crystal – Smoky

Smoky quartz is for water purification.
Master Blend / General Cleanser

When we say that the smoky quartz will purify water, we are speaking about both external bodies of water and the water content in one's physical body. Since we human beings are largely made up of water, this is a very good influence to use in the overall cleansing and balancing process of Rock-Medicine. This vibrational application is also well-applied as an essence twice a day as a preventive measure to avoid toxic buildup as we work to clear the earth's bodies of water. You may put a piece of smoky quartz in a container of water to purify its contents, making it "residue-free" and nontoxic for consumption. You must, however, begin with water that is relatively free from floating pollutants or visibly dense impurities. It is possible to use smoky quartz in emergencies where the only water available is extremely tainted. It is better to use the stone and consume what water is necessary for survival than to endanger one's life due to thirst. The stone requires a three-hour period in the water.

In cases of kidney and bladder failure, the use of smoky quartz is imperative for decreasing the associated toxicity. All conditions of water retention, including water on the brain and water on the knee or elbow, need to be addressed by this stone, either as an essence or in a hand-held application. Likewise, pustules such as water blisters and boils can be administered to by applying a drop or two of essence directly to the eruption. These examples will, of course, be used in their proper combinations.

Influenza is another area in which the smoky quartz will speed the body's elimination of the malady, especially if the patient is consuming ample quantities of liquids, as is the standard practice with flu and colds.

In order to treat bodies of water like pools and ponds, render an essence and dump it directly into the water. For the treatment of vast bodies of water, such as lakes and oceans, smoky quartz may be used in a wand or scepter apparatus, which can be constructed by specific instruction for amplification and focus. This type of instrument is one of the new instances where we are authorized to build crystal and gemstone mechanisms for large-scale treatments. Not many of these setups are needed or authorized, and they must be used very carefully. The reason for this is the intensity of wands and scepters. For example, to point a wand apparatus (not a fluorite) at an individual is akin to going after a small mouse with an atom bomb. That kind of force applied on an individual level is far too powerful and can easily cause damage. Wands are not to be taken lightly or used without specific understanding and instruction.

We are so far from the knowledge of the application of the influence of these instruments that they are not even included by the higher consciousness in this text.

Red Rock of Sedona

Red Rock of Sedona is an invitation to the Holy Spirit to come into one's midst.

This invitation is otherwise known as Iko-Iko, or call and response. The Iko-spirit is that of a ceremonious exchange with the Spirit of Light. In early African times, all tribal dance offerings were preceded with the Iko, as were their meals, ceremonies, and parties. This word found its way through the slave trade to the Cajun bayou area, and its evolution of meanings has come full circle. With a contributing influence on music and rhythm, it is the way to begin all gatherings and celebrations. It honors spiritual exchange.

Iko-Iko is the essence of prayer, forming a simultaneous call and response. When you know to invite the spirit of kindness into your midst, therein you have the proof that it is already there. The state of well-being is sustained by preventing harm or by preventative measures; therein comes protection, and as in all major celebrations, sending out lots of invitations is a big part of ensuring an event's success. No wonder the red rock of invitation is so exciting. The provision of this rock and the knowledge to use it is our own invitation from spirit. We are preparing a place for a jubilee to occur, and it will manifest as the preparations do.

Used by one person, it is a personal invitation to the Holy Spirit to come into that person. When it is included in a long distance spread, it acts as a personal invitation by each and every person within its range. This invitation works equally for everyone, whether they want it, believe it, understand it, know it, or not. It provides a very powerful good, as it is in essence a physical prayer. Knowing to invite the Holy Spirit into our midst is an indication to us that It is already with us. This is prayer answered simultaneously with its request.

Rhodochrosite

Rhodochrosite is for epidermal tissue cells.

This pink-rose-white, soft, layered rock wears the clue to its use on its face. The flesh-pink banding and thin white lines aptly represent the skin tissue that this stone treats. Rhodochrosite can be used for everything from acne to tumors. The vast spectrum includes bites, boils, burns, rashes, eczema, seborrhea, psoriasis, endometriosis, skin grafts, incisions, abrasions, and various other injuries. Rhodochrosite with amethyst and lepidolite are essential elements in treating brain infections with resulting lesions and subsequent adhesions. They are also good for ovarian cysts and adhesions, as well as for treatment of malignant and nonmalignant tumors.

Take care to include all pertinent stones for every distinct area of need.

Rhodonite

Rhodonite is for neurological disorder.

Rhodonite's influence is on the "body electric," our nervous system. Our nerves carry fire and make up our electric body. Nervous disorder manifests itself in a wide range of conditions and chronic disease. There are synapses in the brain and body, the places where nerve cells communicate. Our electricity dances off these neurons. Rhodonite treats neurological disorders in both the brain and the body.

The manifestations of our nervous systems are as individual as our fingerprints. Of particular importance here, when dealing with the structure, messages, and awareness of the nervous system, is the true nature of the symptoms and whether to categorize them as cause or effect. As the cause or catalyst of an imbalance is addressed, we are able to treat in a way that will eradicate the condition from one's being. When we treat merely symptoms or effects of an imbalance, we end up chasing illness after illness around our body. To use moderation or frugality in one's life consists of a reverent sacrifice toward the availability of a clean, pollution-free existence. This means residual-free, toxin-free, and free from blockage of any sort. Free. Through the enactment of this awareness, we assure such a state.

Our neurological communications travel through the most sophisticated routing system imaginable. Single signals can be rapidly exchanged throughout the whole system in fractions of seconds. Just one of these signals gone awry can disrupt the balance of patterning of many areas simultaneously, or right it. Rhodonite seeks out those instances of chemical and/or physiological "misfiring" of the nerve endings and corrects the affected area.

The applications of rhodonite are perfectly suited for "can of worms" type situations where there is no clear-cut source for the malady evident, and where any form of nervous disorder is present. Many psychiatric patients would be better served if the influence of rhodonite is administered, by hand or by essence, for at least three weeks before a conclusive evaluation is done for diagnosis and prognosis.

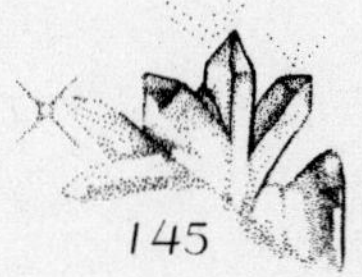

Ruby

Ruby is the physical, mental, and spiritual sex influence.

Ruby derives its name from the blood red color of its appearance. It is one of the most dramatically changed stones from its former use to its current use, that of sexually centered afflictions. Let us begin, first, by stating that the application of ruby is not used in the treatment of AIDS, as AIDS is not the "sexual" disease it has been represented to be. The transmission of this disease has to do with the exchange of body fluids including blood, and not the single element of sexual interaction, as with other so-called sexual infirmities, such as gonorrhea and syphilis. Ruby is used for these two diseases, as well as in the treatment of genital herpes, male contracting of trichinosis, frigidity, inhibitions, and lack of healthy or adequate natural lubrication. Some of the areas less often addressed from their sexual aspects are: recoveries from the traumas of rape, painful intercourse, and inadequate preparation by way of sex education. The ruby also serves as an aphrodisiac. The possibility of its misuse as an aphrodisiac must be considered before adopting the practice. It is always preferable that the use of Rock-Medicine be applied with the knowledge of the patient. Nonetheless, the application of ruby for opening the sexual stimuli channel is one instance where the awareness of the patient may or may not be desired. This is true when there is a lack of candid or comfortable communication between exclusive partners or spouses. Many people have great difficulty in verbalizing their feelings, fears, and preferences to each other when it comes to sexual intimacy. One must not use ruby in this

manner when it is merely to gain the sexual favors of someone who is neither inclined nor predisposed to engage in sexual activity with other than a chosen partner. Our animal attractions to each other are based on subtle chemical reactions. Each one of us will match many people in desire in our lifetimes. Ruby does not cause this attraction to occur. It causes inhibitions and lack of candor to be eliminated so that healthy and open exchange on all levels may take place. Therefore, treat this stone with respect.

Ruby is indicated in another area of sexual clarity, and that is the realm of homosexuality and the lack of one's clarity about their own sexual preference. Bisexual and homosexual tendencies and inclinations are not in themselves maladies. We are speaking exclusively about those individuals who remain confused as to their own desires and preferences, not those men and women who have made comfortable choices and decisions in these areas and who are satisfied with their interpersonal interactions. You can rest assured that when any given situation doesn't feel right, something about it probably isn't. Likewise, when a healthy mind is happy and comfortable in its decision or condition, it is a good indication that the respective interactions are proper for that individual.

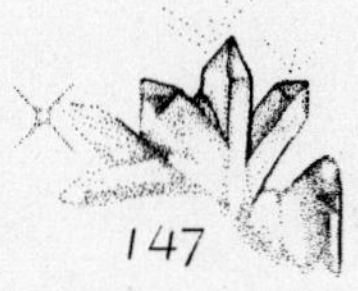

In the event any of the more severe syndromes, such as dangerous sadomasochistic behavior, necrophilia, nymphomania, and/or pedophilia is present, then you must surmise whether the symptoms are cause or effect. Only after this evaluation can you proceed with the relevance of using ruby for the condition.

Selenite

Selenite is for prepubescent fears and traumas.
Master Blend

Selenite, a form of gypsum, treats the child's classic fears of the dark, dogs, nightmares, and bogeymen, but extends far beyond to cover the effects of abuse, incidental traumas, divorce, and death. As adult products of our own childhoods, we can likewise use selenite to treat unresolved issues that occurred when we were children. We can also treat stunted growth patterns on the emotional and mental levels.

We are all children here, and we tend to fight that aspect of our vulnerability. This condition is synonymous with the concept of time. Once life existed gracefully within nature and safely in the fabric of the time-space continuum. Then that fabric "tore," and it tore us away from the universal balance. We have been patching the hole through which ill slips in for thousands of years with a cosmic Band-Aid. The weave is finally bridging the gap between humankind and Mother Earth. This will take us to a space where we are so at one with our environment that we can merge with it and its elements at will. These advanced practices will eliminate the wasteful means of travel and communications. Sounds like the dreams of children to me! Actually, it is science and mathematics and Love's creation of a playground.

Shark's Tooth

Shark's tooth is for the nose, sinus, and nasal passages.

Shark's teeth are readily available. They are collected from the sandy bottom of the ocean. Sharks lose their teeth constantly. The teeth grow in rows which are ever moving forward to replace those missing. In keeping with the spirit of healing this planet as a whole, we do not condone the ravaging of any resource whether it be animal, vegetable, or mineral. Sharks are not killed to provide these instruments.

This instrument is the indicator for the nose. The range of application is vast. For the broken nose you would combine the tooth with coral. For a runny nose or draining sinuses, it would be with fluorite. Any temporary or chronic smelling impairment or sensitivity would be treated with shark's tooth.

Many instances of use will actually be to treat symptoms as in the case of colds, flu, or allergy. Pustules, injuries, and conditions such as a deviated septum are all individualized and will require different combinations.

Whether the affliction is external or internal, shark's tooth identifies the nose as the area in need.

Silver

Silver causes all of the body's meridional, fluid, and energy flows to concentrate at the highest chakra.

The highest chakra is not the top of your head but the topmost point of one's aura. This has been the case since the Harmonic Convergence. From that time, all the cells in your being, from essence to aura, are chakras. The literal topmost chakra is the "highest" in all respects. It is physically located at the highest part of your being and is the closest in proximity to the higher consciousness.

First, we will address the safeguards to be taken into account when using silver. Silver is not conducive to being worn safely at all times, especially by women. The primary reason for this is that the menstrual flow is a lower-body elimination. Since the action of silver's influence is to raise all flows to the uppermost chakra area, its presence is contraindicated when the female system is attempting to send the monthly blood release to the lowest body orifice. This effect can certainly be a contributing factor to those who experience cramping during this period. The body's attempts to pursue a downward flow are inhibited by the upward pull of the presence of silver, causing conflictive energies and the resulting cramping in the middle body area. Another condition that is acted upon counterproductively by silver, in either men or women, is the presence of either bladder or kidney infection. This is again a circumstance where the body's attempts at lower-body elimination become inhibited by the upward-pulling influence of the silver, the danger being the constant reinfection of the already ailing area and the ultimate weakening of one's natural healing response.

Conditions resulting in the retention of excess body fluids of all types are all worsened by the presence of silver, when it is either held or worn by the individual. (This includes the use of real silverware used during a meal.)

This brings us to the proper uses of silver. In many situations, the preferred concentration of energy flow is toward the highest chakra. One such example is the case of incontinence, or lack of bladder control. The constant application of silver in this instance would quickly produce high levels of toxicity, but for temporary protection from an embarrassing accident at a particular function or social event, one may use silver for a period of up to six hours to aid in the freedom from leakage or seepage. Likewise, in the event that a woman is at risk during pregnancy by either dropping too soon or losing her water, silver with mother-of-pearl can be administered daily in the standard application of an essence to strengthen the conflict caused by the gravitational pull.

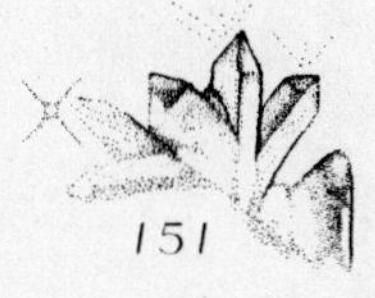

Silver is also an excellent choice for combining with any stones conducive to the higher studies, to help concentrate the thought processes as mental and/or spiritual consciousness. For example, one may use the hessonite garnet (jacinth) to promote higher visions of inspired quality, or when doing specific work with the chrysocolla for formal academic pursuits of a metaphysical nature. These uses are only for those times where the situations and conditions of safeguards have been observed.

At no time is lapis lazuli ever to be set in silver for any purpose, because the strengthening of one's spirit is a total-being function, and to concentrate this influential combination at the highest chakra will very quickly "amp out" the conscious presence of mind, and certain aspects of delusion and narcissism will result. (See **Lapis Lazuli**.)

The emotional attachment to objects worn of silver does not negate these standards.

Sodalite

Sodalite is for celebration.
Master Blend / Shield Stone

Sometimes confused with lapis because of its blue coloring, sodalite is generally softer than lapis (lapis can usually be identified by the presence of gold-colored iron pyrite). In using a stone whose influence is that of celebration, don't limit the possibilities. It is effective in opening the awareness up to the knowledge that Lovelight has got us all and that everything is covered—well-covered.

There can be times when joy, elation, and clarity can be so overwhelming that one nearly faints. I wish for each one of us to experience such rapture that we are beside ourselves! Believe me—it happens. When in the course of delighting in your work and gatherings and celebrations, increase the use of sodalite, to give you a more extensive containment capacity. As events unfold, those of us who are prepared must be of assistance to those who are reacting with panic and fear. Sodalite is for when you feel the need to celebrate, yet you've got so much to do that you must have help staying on track to complete the work at hand. We will be needed to bring in calm as the new reality sets in.

Sugelite

Sugelite is for self-discipleship.
Master Blend / Shield Stone

Sugelite is a beautiful purple stone that comes predominantly from Africa. It can range in color from a marbling of purples to a very dark, almost black, plum color. Self-discipleship is very close to self-control; however, it is not so militant a concept as self-discipline. The additional quality in self-discipleship is Love, wherein Love of yourself becomes synonymous with the Love of all others. The results create a daily dedication to see to the needs of all.

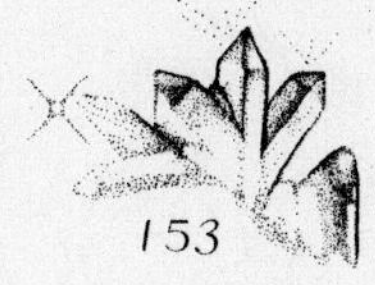

A very basic place to use sugelite is in individuals who are slack-natured toward healthy routine—people who have a tendency not to take, or not to take all, or not to take as directed, prescribed therapies and medicines. This is particularly true of instances where the disease is not life-threatening or alarming enough to the patient.

Obviously, due to the nature of difficulty in administering to themselves, it is best to do a spread or to put essence in all the beverage products in the house that may be safely consumed. This is not a stone to be used for extreme need only! We would all do well to have higher levels of true self-discipleship. Try sugelite when you are finding it hard to eat and exercise properly, for it combines the influences of discipline and nurturing. Sugelite represents an active dedication to a higher quality of life.

Sulfur

Sulfur is for inflammation and swelling of connective joint and muscle tissue.

This is the stone for arthritis and bursitis. It is used with halite in the treatment and prevention of atrophy in coma, paralysis, and in geriatric patients. The four standard applications all apply. For immediate relief of swelling and inflammation, sulfur may be held directly on the affected area.

Certain safeguards must be observed in the use of sulfur and sulfite. (They are interchangeable.) Due to the water-soluble nature of this mineral, we do not make an essence out of it, because residuals would remain in the water. Therefore, always use a set crystal. Sulfur must be kept off of mucous membranes and open wounds, as it will burn. This is an additional reason for not making an essence out of sulfur itself or using it in a bath. Ingested sulfur can be extremely toxic.

Sulfur is a valuable first-aid tool for application to sprains and wrenchings. It is also good assistance for whiplash injuries. It is used for the loss of muscle control, again with halite, in such conditions as muscular dystrophy. The full treatment of all conditions includes—you guessed it—the Master Blend!

Sulfur can be brittle and fragile. Since the applications are always external, the handling of the stone can create much wear and tear, therefore, sulfur is a good candidate for setting as a clear quartz crystal, for use in topical applications.

Talc

Talc is for use during regression work.

Talc is commonly used to make baby powder, bath powder, foot powder, and facial make-up powder. Talc is multidimensional in its prime role as the facilitator of past-life and time regression. It is for clarity of facts and information. It adds comfort, ease, and protection during past-life or time trances. Talc does not bring one into a regressed state, but rather is for help and clarity during such a trance state, once induced. Talc allows the patient to be first-person present during the regression, with conscious knowledge that the events experienced are not happening in real time and need not be hurtful.

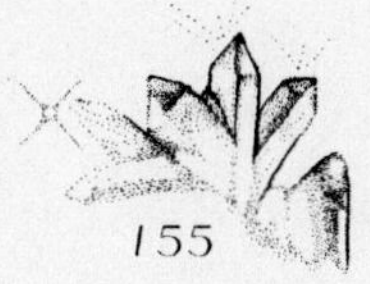

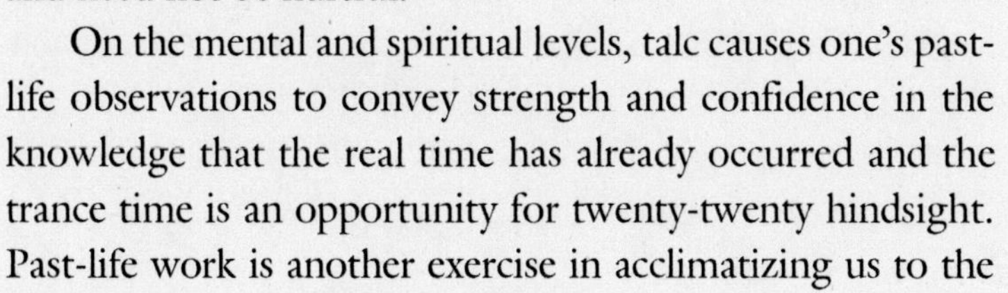

On the mental and spiritual levels, talc causes one's past-life observations to convey strength and confidence in the knowledge that the real time has already occurred and the trance time is an opportunity for twenty-twenty hindsight. Past-life work is another exercise in acclimatizing us to the ideas of the everlasting and infinite.

Tiger's Eye

Tiger's eye is for fatigue.

Tiger's eye is not meant to be used to replace needed sleep, but rather to serve as a "shot in the arm" for those times when monotony and tedium set in. Tiger's eye is held in the appropriate right or left hand, for ten to fifteen minutes. It gives an immediate energy boost, whether the need is physical, mental, or spiritual. Long waits, especially with children, and certainly when traveling, are two excellent examples of standard use. At a long function or event, or when you need a "second wind," tiger's eye is most helpful.

It is a good stone to keep with you for others and a great introduction to the use of Rock-Medicine.

Tiger's eye comes in many colors. Be sure the pieces you acquire are not heat or chemical treated.

Topaz

Topaz changes negative energy to positive.
Master Blend / Shield Stone

We are not speaking here of the electromagnetic or polar concepts of negative and positive; it is the "good" versus "bad" that we mean. There are three stones that everyone should have on themselves at all times: agate, diamond, and topaz. If it were possible to get only one stone in the hand of every individual, planet-wide, at the same moment, if it were topaz, then we would have heaven on earth in an instant. This may sound like an impossibility, but I believe it is more easily accomplished than getting us all of one mind or belief.

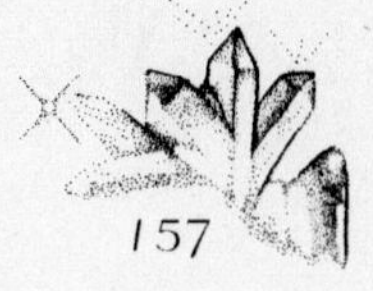

There are three main colors of topaz. In terms of optimal use, the blue is for those in clinical or medical professions. The yellow is for those who teach and/or practice metaphysics. The smoky is for the general public. You may certainly use any color you like for yourself. This is just a guideline of optimal application for those in the first two categories.

Agate, diamond, and topaz do not get toxic; they are shields and can be worn constantly. One suggestion is to have an item of jewelry made with diamond and topaz in it, preferably in brass or gold. Remember that the size and quality of the stones is unimportant, as long as they are true representations of their mineral family. Take care not to use heat or chemical treated stones.

Topaz causes the negative or ailing vibrations at every level to be dissipated, and the void that is left is filled in by the surrounding influence, which is the positive.

Tourmaline

Tourmalines do individual tasks based upon their individual colors.

Green tourmaline is for the treatment of blood sugar imbalance. It does not matter if the condition is diabetic or hypoglycemic. The green works to bring the level from either direction into balance. If a person is insulin-dependent, it is required that diopside be added. It can't be reiterated enough times that you must set up a complete sentence when using stones, for they refer to each other for directing their application. The Master Blend is always necessary when treating any blood sugar disorder. If glaucoma or kidney failure are threatened or present, add malachite to the combination for the eyes or yellow/orange calcite to indicate the kidney area. These are done in separate combinations and applications. All of the possible combinations for the various maladies are not given in this book; instead, sporadic examples are given to help you surmise what are proper and complete combinations.

Next is **black tourmaline**. This is for the lung's interior surface. It is for removing or "scraping" foreign particles off the tissues and cilia. Some examples are the airborne residues found in smog and other air pollution. Do not confuse the use of black tourmaline with that of rough fluorite, which is for fluid and mucus substances in the lungs. However, they may be indicated for use together. Black tourmaline is applied in cases of black lung and other occupational or accidental circumstances where one has breathed toxic gasses, fumes, and irritant materials. On the other hand, if there is a deterioration of the lung interior surface area, this tourmaline builds it back up with the help of rhodochrosite and amethyst. It is added to the combination for cancer when the lungs are involved.

Watermelon tourmaline is the gatekeeper for all the tourmalines. Pink tourmaline and watermelon tourmaline are the same in Rock-Medicine. The gatekeeper is needed because of the tourmaline's extreme nature in its ability to work in either direction. Watermelon, or pink, is what keeps the diabetic's sugar level stopped at the balance point as opposed to continuing on toward hypoglycemia. Also, it prevents the black tourmaline from scraping the lung's interior so harshly that it injures or removes the protective cilia. It is suggested that those who are in the habit of wearing the green or black tourmaline get a pink one set into the same piece of jewelry or to wear as a separate piece at the same time. This ensures against throwing these areas out of balance. The Rock-Medicine safeguards are few but very important.

Turquoise

Turquoise is a symbolic stone representing the wisdom of the ancients.

The currently active resonant tool for work or treatment in the area of knowledge and education is chrysocolla. Turquoise is in effect "retired" and serves as a reminder to all that humankind has endured and expedited to bring us to this point in time. It sits with the crystal ball as a memorial rather than an active instrument. The crystal ball serves to remind us of the "all is one" reality. The turquoise has earned a place of honor and pays homage to the last culture in modern times to keep alive the concept of this planet as a living entity—the Native American peoples.

Ulexite

Ulexite is for infidelity.
Men's Hormonal Balance

Ulexite combines with citrine and bornite for male hormone imbalance. When we speak of infidelity, we are not limiting our understanding of the word to marital or monogamous arrangements. Infidelity is equally applicable to any situation where one is not being true to the family unit. The father who divorces and does not continue to pursue a full relationship with the children, the siblings who spend years on end in a grudge feud, or the daughter who disowns her mother and vice versa are all good examples. Use this stone any time that a member of an immediate family unit, whether born of the bloodline or not, has closed the door of candid and healthy exchange or communication with other members of the unit. This is infidelity. Interestingly, ulexite is also known as the TV stone for its fiber-optic quality and appearance.

Wood Opal

Wood opal is for the ears.

Whether used in the treatment of infection, the loss of hearing ability, or even a mental listening block, wood opal is equally applicable when added to the proper Rock-Medicine sentence. Rock-Medicine is a form of science and will elicit amazing, miracle-like responses in many cases. It is, however, a technology and does have its limitations. There are no examples where Rock-Medicine has restored vision to the blind or hearing to the deaf.

Some good applications are to those whose life puts them in situations where very loud noise does continuous damage. This can be music, machinery, or crowd noise. It is, of course, advisable always to act responsibly by engaging preventative measures, such as ear protection. Wood opal will work to counter any damage already sustained.

Many children, as well as adults, suffer from recurrent ear infection. When used with the cleansers, wood opal fights, as well as prevents, these infections. For circumstances of fluid in the ears, add fluorite. Several balancc problems are related to inner ear disorders, and wood opal may be used for these.

This stone can even be used for those who have trouble listening.

For use with higher level study, you might combine the red rock of Sedona with the diamond and wood opal to set up a combination for hearing the voice of the spirit, or with sugelite to listen to your own heart's desires.

Wulfenite

Wulfenite is for trauma to the head area.

Any type of blow to the head is treated with wulfenite. Concussion, whether it is light or severe, needs wulfenite. This stone also works retroactively for the treatment of an old head injury.

Some specific examples of application are the victims of accidents or abuse. Wulfenite prevents the long term effects of swelling and bruising, as well as blood clotting and tumor. Wulfenite says "head" in any sentence you set up with it. Sometimes you may need to include lepidolite, to indicate brain trauma involvement. As lepidolite works on the brain chemical imbalance, wulfenite works on the head. Adding coral to wulfenite says "head bone," which is the skull. With amethyst, rhodochrosite, and moldavite it may indicate a fungus, or with rhodochrosite and amethyst, it combats skin problems on the scalp.

Any time there is surgery in the head area, wulfenite is essential to the healing process. In the treatment of a chronic migraine headache, try jade, amber, and wulfenite. You may add chrysoprase for the pain, as long as you know the cause of the headache. If that cause is stress, use petrified wood in addition.

Remember to use the Master Blend always, as a foundation for your specifics.

Afterword: The Great Work

Multitudes of volumes have been written on these changing times. Some call this period one of planetary transition. We are talking about simple and basic change. Humankind has already begun to swing the value system or the quality of life toward an enlightened existence, due to the overwhelming desire of the masses for peace. With this desire comes an automatic response to the plight of those unfortunates who are without water, food, shelter, and clothing. Ever-increasing numbers of individuals are rising to contribute to meet these needs of others near and far.

Just as the single child is getting the assistance it needs to grow in a productive manner, so too has the very planet received "care packages" of information to expedite the salvation of its growth and well-being.

Rock-Medicine is the means by which all things toxic may be cleared to their states of balance.

We are all connected by way of mind, body, and spirit. Although we can do all things by way of our minds' powers and abilities, we must be in top working order to do so. This makes the wellness of each one of us the responsibility of us all. In other words, where there is found one brother or sister among you who has an illness or imbalance, so also have you. This realization takes the idea of health care out of the previous and cumbersome realm of confidentiality.

Rock-Medicine has the unique quality of being able to be administered effectively to another whether or not they accept it, want it, believe it, or know it. This clinical application for the ills and ailments of others is but one aspect of the cleanup measures known as the Great Work. From a place of well-being come inclinations toward turning the tide away from current waste and abuse of the earth and its resources.

There are no exceptions to the rule that all are in need of healing, just as there are no exceptions to the fact that the health of all is the responsibility of us all.

Foremost in the path of enlightenment is the realization that all elements given by and derived from the Mother Earth have a purpose. All things are tools and instruments set here for our use. A high degree of misuse exists regarding a great number of these, due to a lack of proper knowledge of application. We hide from being our brother/sister's keeper. Most of the things we do are state-altering, whether it be watching TV or ingesting chemicals, chanting, dancing, or merely breathing. We see much in the way of denial of the reality of our world's situation. So many people abuse drugs and alcohol, using them as crutches and hiding places, rather than in their intended capacity as a means of enhancing celebration and of altering perspectives to expand creativity.

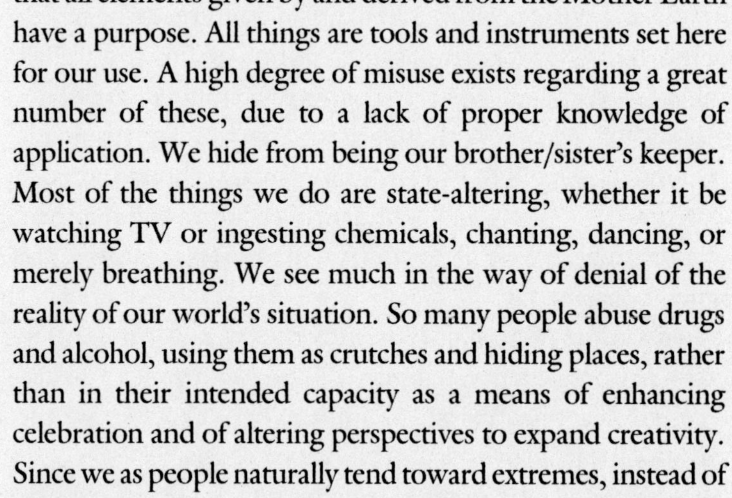

Since we as people naturally tend toward extremes, instead of learning moderation in the use of these powerful influences, we have developed the equal and opposite mentality that total abstinence is the only answer. This "baby-proofing" scenario holds control of our own lives at bay, just as does the ignorance of overindulgence. In other words, to use or not use any mode of mind-altering tool should be a decision based on evaluation and choice, and not one of fear. This guideline is a point of reference that can be applied to a vast number of other areas, inclusive of incantations, meditations, foodstuffs, and of being our brother's keeper. Religious indoctrination is based equally in fear and denial of one's connection to the whole. True freedom is the love of making moment-to-moment decisions based upon the moment-to-moment changes in the personal environment. This allows flow.

The Great Work is the detoxification of the planet's mind, body, and spirit, as well as our own. This is necessary to allow the Creator's divine presence to return and fully abide with this plane on a full-time basis, thus giving back to us our state of grace, or Heaven on Earth.

The list of available stones and their uses is self-explanatory as to what is required in the way of addressing the imbalance of our current existence. First, of course, are the obvious individual cases of medical need. Next, we have to deal with the dangerous level of radiation toxicity planetwide. For this, we can set up systems of long-distance spreads using covellite. Next, we can treat the air pollution, for which we use pyrite. This again is where we administer by way of a long-distance spread. Water pollution is going to take a bit more preparation and involvement. To get the stones' vibrations in the necessary form for application, we must first render an essence of smoky quartz in some contained water, and then add the essence to the bodies of water and systems. In order to obtain and then maintain a nontoxic environment, it will be optimal to utilize our current advances in technology to set a vast long-distance spread in orbit around the planet. These applications are some of the first steps in the cleansing process. We must next take measures to prevent the reintroduction of the toxins. This will obviously require the assistance, cooperation, and large-scale involvement by the governments of the Earth. This can only be expected when the true scientific nature of the practice and studies of Rock-Medicine are adopted by the masses. This awareness is coming in rapidly. Your participation by way of the use of this domestic text for the health and improvement of your households and communities will facilitate its manifestation.

Appendices

Use Guide by Stone

Abalone	domestic maturity
Adamite	elimination of blame
Agate	first aid, rescue, and guardian angel
Alexandrite	adapting to change from patriarchal to matriarchal system
Amazonite	judgment
Amber	memory/DNA structure; memory of wellness
Amethyst	cell division and alcohol detoxification
Apatite	metabolization of nutrients
Aquamarine	mouth
Aragonite	community unity
Aventurine	elimination of prejudice
Azurite	self-healing, dream enhancement
Azurite/Malachite	paranoid schizophrenia
Barite	fungi
Beryl	awakening the psyche
Bloodstone	HIV virus
Bornite	arrogance
Calcite	cancer
Carnelian	blood purifier for age 55 and older
Celestite	truth
Chalcedony	shield system
Chrysocolla	comprehension, education, matriarch
Chrysoprase	pain
Cinnabar	heart strength
Citrine	irritability
Clay	detoxification of immune system
Coal	self-esteem
Coral	regenerative purification and strengthening of bone and calcium
Covellite	radiation toxicity
Diamond	conscious harmony and balance
Dinosaur Bone	eliminates waste

Emerald	back area
Fluorite	unwanted fluids
Fluorite Wands	impressionable for specific healing influences
Galena	balanced breathing
Garnet	blood pressure
Gold	strength
Granite	kindness and gentleness
Halite	muscles
Hematite	blood purifier for ages 55 and under
Hemimorphite	transformation
Herkimer Diamond	throat, larynx, voice box, and vocal chords
Iolite	bone marrow
Ivory	infertility
Jacinth/Hessonite Garnet	creative visualization
Jade	detoxification of emotional, physical, and spiritual residues
Jasper	shield for positive outcomes
Kunzite	surrender
Lapis	strengthening of spirit, transmitter
Lava	command of authority
Lepidolite	brain
Magnetite	reversing the polarity of a situation
Malachite	eyes
Moldavite	fungus-related imbalances
Moonstone *(Labradorite)*	PMS-related syndromes and regular monthly upset
Mother-of-Pearl	strengthening of womb
Obsidian	prophecy
Onyx	shielding from intense energy exchange
Opal	elimination of fear or denial of divine calling
Pearl	female reproductive system and nurturing
Peridot	for changes in enlightenment

Petrified Wood — stress
Pyrite — air purification
Quartz Crystal
  Clear — amplification
  Rose — comfort and joy at times of sorrow over loss
  Smoky — water purification
Red Rock of Sedona — invitation for Holy Spirit to enter
Rhodochrosite — epidermal tissue cells
Rhodonite — neurological disorder
Ruby — sex influence
Selenite — children's phobias and traumas
Shark's Tooth — sinus and nasal passages
Silver — raises flow of energy upward
Sodalite — celebration
Sugelite — self-discipleship
Sulfur — inflammation and swelling of connective joint and muscle tissue
Talc — regression work
Tiger's Eye — fatigue
Topaz — changing negative energy to positive
Tourmalines
  Green — blood sugar imbalance
  Black — lungs interior surface
  Watermelon/Pink — gatekeeper for balance
Turquoise — symbolic of wisdom of the ancients
Ulexite — infidelity
Wood Opal — ears
Wulfenite — head

Use Guide for Specific Conditions

You may add stones to the Master Blend, as indicated by the following list of applications. Where no additional stones are indicated, the Master Blend itself is the complete application. A colon is used to indicate that the stones listed are to be added to the specific application (e.g., see below, Allergies, Cancer, etc.).

Acne	amethyst, fluorite, rhodochrosite
Adhesions	amethyst, halite, rhodochrosite
Aggression	aragonite, bornite
AIDS	amethyst, heliotrope (bloodstone)
Alcoholism	amethyst
Allergies	amethyst, galena:
Eyes	fluorite, malachite
Nose	fluorite, sharks tooth
Rash	rhodochrosite
Alzheimer's	amethyst, lepidolite, rhodonite
Anemia	amethyst, apatite
Angina	amethyst, cinnabar, garnet, chrysoprase
Anorexia	amethyst, apatite
Anxiety	Master Blend
Arthritis	halite, sulfur, amethyst, chrysoprase
Asthma	amethyst, galena, black tourmaline, pink or watermelon tourmaline
Atrophy	amethyst, halite
Blood pressure	amethyst, cinnabar, garnet
Bone damage	amethyst, coral
Brain	amethyst, lepidolite:
Chemical imbalance	Master Blend
Fluid on	fluorite
Neurological	rhodonite
Tumor	rhodochrosite

Bronchitis	amethyst, galena, black tourmaline, watermelon or pink tourmaline
Burns	amethyst, rhodochrosite (immediate topical application of honey!)
Bursitis	amethyst, fluorite, sulfur, chrysoprase
Calcium deposits	amethyst, coral
Cancer	amethyst, rhodochrosite, chrysoprase:
Bladder	yellow or orange calcite
Bone	white or clear calcite, iolite
Breast	blue calcite, pearl
Cervical	white calcite, pearl
Colon	apatite, green calcite
Kidney	yellow or orange calcite
Leukemia	pink or red calcite
Liver	green calcite
Lung	white calcite, black tourmaline, watermelon or pink tourmaline
Lymphoma	blue calcite
Ovarian	white calcite, pearl
Pancreas	yellow or orange calcite
Prostate	yellow or orange calcite
Skin	white calcite
Spleen	green calcite
Stomach	apatite, green calcite
Candida	amethyst, barite, moldavite
Cardiac	amethyst, cinnabar, halite
Cataracts	amethyst, coral, malachite
Complexion	amethyst, rhodochrosite
Concussion	amethyst, lepidolite, rhodochrosite, wulfenite
Conjunctivitis (pink eye)	amethyst, fluorite, malachite Make essence & drop in each eye four times daily.
Cuts	amethyst, rhodochrosite (immediate topical application of honey!)

Dental	aquamarine, amethyst:
Abscess	fluorite, rhodochrosite
Gums	rhodocrosite
Teeth	coral
Depression	amethyst, lepidolite
Diabetes	amethyst, green tourmaline, pink or watermelon tourmaline:
Insulin dependent	diopside
Divorce trauma	ruby
Domesticity	abalone, aragonite, ulexite
Insecurity	Master Blend
Ears	amethyst, wood opal
Eating disorders	apatite
Emphysema	amethyst, galena, black tourmaline, watermelon or pink tourmaline
Endometriosis	amethyst, pearl, rhodochrosite
Epilepsy	amethyst, lepidolite
Fatigue	tiger's eye
Fear	azurite, malachite
Female hormone balance	amethyst, pearl
Fever	amethyst
Flu	amethyst, chrysoprase:
For treating individual symptoms:	
Ear	wood opal
Nose	shark's tooth
Throat	Herkimer diamond
Stomach	green calcite
Fluid	amethyst, fluorite:
Elbow	sulfur
Knee	sulfur
Lungs	black tourmaline, watermelon or pink tourmaline
Retention	apatite
Frigidity	ruby, pearl

General physical cleansing	amethyst
Goiter	amethyst, Herkimer diamond, blue calcite
Grief	Master Blend
Headache	Master Blend
Hemophilia	amethyst, garnet
Hepatitis	amethyst
Herpes	amethyst, rhodochrosite
HIV	amethyst, heliotrope
Impotence	amethyst, bornite, ulexite, ruby
Infertility	ivory, ruby:
Physical	amethyst, pearl
Emotional	Master Blend
Infidelity	ulexite
Inflammation	amethyst:
Joints	sulfur
Muscle	halite
Insecurity	Master Blend
Inspiration	hessonite garnet, obsidian, red beryl
Irritability	Master Blend
Itching	amethyst, rhodochrosite
Lack of Kindness	Master Blend
Larynx	amethyst, Herkimer diamond
Male hormone balance	amethyst, bornite, ulexite
Menopause	amethyst, pearl
Mononucleosis	amethyst, tiger's eye
Multiple sclerosis	amethyst, rhodonite
Muscles	amethyst, halite
Muscular dystrophy	amethyst, halite
Neurological disorders	amethyst, rhodonite:
Back	emerald
Body	rhodocrosite
Brain	lepidolite
Nightmares	Master Blend

Obesity	amethyst, apatite, rhodochrosite
Osteoporosis	amethyst, coral, emerald
Ovarian Cysts	amethyst, pearl, rhodochrosite
Pain	chrysoprase as appropriate
Pleurisy	amethyst, fluorite, black tourmaline, watermelon or pink tourmaline
PMS	pearl:
Bloating	amethyst, fluorite
Cramping	chrysoprase
Irritability	Master Blend
Pneumonia	amethyst, fluorite, black tourmaline, watermelon or pink tourmaline
Prejudice	Master Blend
Prenatal care	amethyst, mica:
Brain chemicals	lepidolite
Bone development	coral
Heart	cinnabar
Prepubescent trauma	Master Blend:
Sexual	ruby
Radiation toxicity	amethyst
Rape trauma	ruby
Schizophrenia	azurite, malachite
Self-control	Master Blend
Self-esteem	Master Blend
Spine	amethyst, coral, emerald
Stress	Master Blend
Suicidal tendencies	magnetite
Throat	amethyst, Herkimer diamond
Thyroid	amethyst, blue calcite, Herkimer diamond
Truthfulness	Master Blend
Vertigo	amethyst, wood opal
Vocal chords	amethyst, Herkimer diamond
Voice box	amethyst, Herkimer diamond
Wastefulness	Master Blend

Cautions and Safeguards

The precautions in Rock-Medicine are relatively few. Most have been previously indicated in this text and are summarized here. Always seek a diagnosis from a credible clinician. When taking prescribed medicines, you must seek frequent review by your physician so that levels of medications can be monitored and adjusted. NEVER ingest any part or portion of any mineral described in this text. Do not use water soluble stones, or any stone appearing to have a less than stable density, for making an essence or hand holding, rather use a set crystal. Follow all standards and guidelines as described in this text.

Stone	Caution	Safeguard
Amethyst	Never to be worn or used alone, except in your glass when drinking alcohol (causes cell mitosis and intensifies injuries)	Use with specific stones to address changes and healing of cell structure
Chrysoprase	Pain serves a purpose in indicating the presence of damage	Do not use without knowledge of what is causing pain
Cinnabar	Mercury toxic, water soluble	Do not touch, hand-hold, or ingest. Employ only when set to a quartz crystal. Wipe quartz thoroughly.
Fluorite Wands	Predisposed by thought or word to a specific purpose	Be sure you are using them for the purpose they have been set for.
Galena	Water soluble and lead toxic	Do not use in essence (make a set crystal)

Halite	Water soluble	Do not use in essence (make a set crystal)
Lapis Lazuli	Strengthens one's current spirit, for good or ill effect	Evaluate carefully the "spirit" you are about to amplify. Set lapis only in gold; avoid contact with silver and other metals.
Lepidolite	Lithium-based, water soluble	Do not use in essence (make a set crystal)
Magnetite	Water soluble	Do not use in essence (make a set crystal)
Quartz	Amplifies whatever vibration it contacts	Be conscious of what your quartz is in a position to amplify.
Silver	Pulls all flows strongly upward	Avoid using during menses, kidney or bladder infections, diarrhea, etc. Do not wear when attempting to do a cleansing.
Sulfur/sulfite	Toxic and water soluble	Do not use in essence (make a set crystal)

How to Order Stones

While most "rock shops" will have many of the stones required for making formulas, we have found that Olympic Mountain Gems, Inc. is a quality, one-stop source for most gems, crystals, and stones available worldwide. Please feel free to contact them for ordering the Master Blend, Seven Cleansers, or any Special Combinations.

Olympic Mountain Gems, Inc.
640 Bay Street
Port Orchard, WA 98366
Phone: 360 895-9344
Fax: 360 874-9352
www.omgems.com

Rock Reference Guides

Theseselect reference books, and many others, are generally available at finer rock shops, or at your library. For a more complete list of books on rocks, gems, crystals, and minerals, see http://www.omgems.com.

Arem, Joel. *Rocks and Minerals.* $12.00

Kraus, Barry. *Mineral Collector's Handbook.* $24.95

Schumann, Walter. *Gemstones of the World.* Sterling Publishing. $24.95

Schumann, Walter. *Minerals of the World.* Sterling Publishing. $19.95